TARGE' MATHS

Year 3

Stephen Pearce

Elmwood Press

First published 2002 by
Elmwood Press
80 Attimore Road
Welwyn Garden City
Herts. AL8 6LP
Tel. 01707 333232

British Library Cataloguing in Publication Data

Pearce, Stephen

    1. Mathematics—1961–
    I. Title

ISBN 1 902 214 218

Numerical answers are published in a separate book

Typeset and illustrated by Tech-Set Ltd., Gateshead, Tyne and Wear
Printed and bound by WS Bookwell.

PREFACE

Target Maths has been written for pupils in Year 3 and their teachers.

The intention of the book is to provide teachers with material to teach *all* the NNS objectives, as set out in the yearly teaching programme, with *all* the children in their class able to work at their appropriate level of ability.

One of the key principles for the approach to teaching recommended by the NNS is 'controlled differentiation, with all pupils engaged in mathematics related to a common theme.' **Target Maths** is structured so that controlled differentiation is built into every lesson. How a teacher decides to use the material would depend upon the children's familiarity with the topic and the amount of time that is available.

Each lesson in the book is divided into four sections. The four sections are:

- The introduction: a clearly stated learning intention and, where necessary, explanations and examples of new work.
- Section A: activities based upon the NNS expected learning outcomes for Year 2 pupils. This section can be used to remind children of work previously covered, as well as providing material for the less confident child.
- Section B: activities based upon the NNS expected learning outcomes for Year 3 pupils. Most children should be able to work successfully at this level.
- Section C: activities based upon the NNS expected learning outcomes for Year 4 pupils. This section provides extension material for the faster workers and for those who need to be moved quickly onto more challenging tasks. Problems in Section C can also provide useful material for discussion in the plenary session.

The correspondence of the three sections to the NNS learning outcomes expected of different year groups provides a simple, manageable framework for both the formal and informal assessment of children's progress. The expectations in the yearly teaching programmes correspond to these National Curriculum levels.

- Section A   Year 2   consolidation of level 2, start on level 3
- Section B   Year 3   revision of level 2, but mainly level 3
- Section C   Year 4   consolidation of level 3, start on level 4

Both the NNS Teaching Programme for Year 3 and the Term Framework are in the Answer Book with **Target Maths** page references for all the NNS objectives.

The author is indebted to many colleagues who have assisted him in this work. He is particularly grateful to David Rayner and Sharon Granville for their invaluable advice and support.

CONTENTS

On these pages you will learn to read and write whole numbers.

You will need to know and use these words:

1 one	8 eight	15 fifteen	30 thirty
2 two	9 nine	16 sixteen	40 forty
3 three	10 ten	17 seventeen	50 fifty
4 four	11 eleven	18 eighteen	60 sixty
5 five	12 twelve	19 nineteen	70 seventy
6 six	13 thirteen	20 twenty	80 eighty
7 seven	14 fourteen	21 twenty-one	90 ninety

The way we read a digit depends upon its position in the number.

Examples

27 reads 'twenty-seven'

274 reads 'two hundred and seventy-four'

2745 reads 'two thousand seven hundred and forty-five'

A

The children in Class 3A have been writing their addresses.
Write these house numbers in figures.

1 Chris   – thirteen
2 Matthew – sixteen
3 Sarah   – forty-nine
4 Claire   – seventy-two
5 David   – three hundred

6 Emma – twelve
7 Laura – fifteen
8 Daniel – fifty-eight
9 Andy   – thirty-seven
10 Becky – ninety

Write each of these children's house numbers in words.

11 Gemma
(14)

12 Rachel
(18)

13 Kelly
(26)

14 Andrew
(95)

15 Simon
(60)

16 Michael
(17)

17 Vicky
(19)

18 Mark
(83)

19 Katie
(500)

20 Ryan
(1000)

21 Jenny
(32)

22 Marcus
(200)

B

Write the numbers of these raffle tickets in words.

1 43   3 176   5 238   7 424   9 317

2 789   4 52   6 540   8 635   10 861

The prize winning numbers were called out. Draw the tickets.

11 Sixty-five.

12 One hundred and forty-two.

13 Five hundred and ninety-four.

14 Four hundred and sixty.

15 Seventy-seven.

16 Two hundred and fifty-one.

17 Eight hundred and twelve.

18 Six hundred and nine.

19 One hundred and eighty.

20 Nine hundred and eighty-four.

C

Write the heights of these mountains in words.

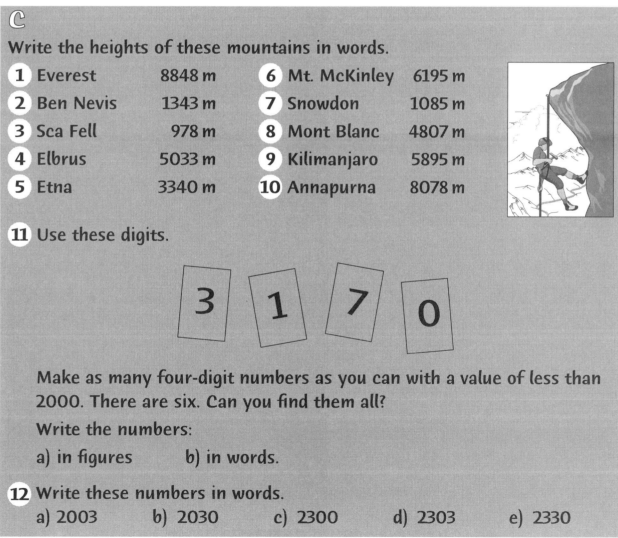

1 Everest   8848 m

2 Ben Nevis   1343 m

3 Sca Fell   978 m

4 Elbrus   5033 m

5 Etna   3340 m

6 Mt. McKinley 6195 m

7 Snowdon   1085 m

8 Mont Blanc   4807 m

9 Kilimanjaro 5895 m

10 Annapurna   8078 m

11 Use these digits.

3 1 7 0

Make as many four-digit numbers as you can with a value of less than 2000. There are six. Can you find them all?

Write the numbers:

a) in figures   b) in words.

12 Write these numbers in words.

a) 2003   b) 2030   c) 2300   d) 2303   e) 2330

On these pages you will learn to count on and back in 1s, 10s and 100s.

Examples

Count on 6 in 1s from 128.

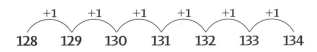

Count back 6 in 1s from 452.

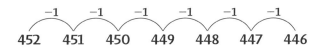

Count on 60 in 10s from 871.

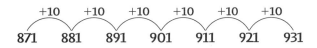

Count back 60 in 10s from 237.

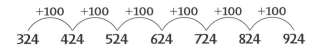

Count on 600 in 100s from 324.

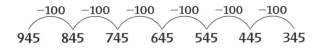

Count back 600 in 100s from 945.

$$945 \quad 845 \quad 745 \quad 645 \quad 545 \quad 445 \quad 345$$

A

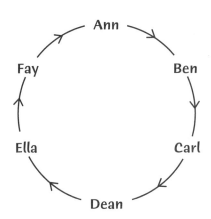

Six children practise counting in a circle.

Counting on in 10s.
1 Carl starts at 40.
   Who says 80?
2 Fay starts at 26.
   Who says 76?
3 Ann starts at 38.
   Who says 98?

Counting back in 1s.
4 Ben starts at 37.
   Who says 32?
5 Dean starts at 99.
   Who says 93?
6 Fay starts at 58.
   Who says 51?

Counting back in 10s.
7 Ella starts at 70.
   Who says 20?
8 Ben starts at 95.
   Who says 35?
9 Dean starts at 84.
   Who says 14?

B

Count back in 1s.
1. 6 from 124
2. 8 from 156
3. 9 from 183
4. 12 from 218

Count on in 10s.
5. 40 from 635
6. 50 from 180
7. 60 from 256
8. 70 from 374

Count back in 100s.
9. 300 from 750
10. 400 from 980
11. 500 from 639
12. 600 from 873

Copy and complete.
13. 166 167 168 169 ☐ ☐ ☐
14. 250 260 270 280 ☐ ☐ ☐
15. 330 320 310 300 ☐ ☐ ☐
16. 262 362 462 562 ☐ ☐ ☐
17. 236 237 238 239 ☐ ☐ ☐
18. 465 475 485 495 ☐ ☐ ☐
19. 547 537 527 517 ☐ ☐ ☐
20. 730 630 530 430 ☐ ☐ ☐
21. ☐ ☐ ☐ 152 153 154 155
22. ☐ ☐ ☐ 411 421 431 441
23. ☐ ☐ ☐ 315 415 515 615
24. ☐ ☐ ☐ 802 803 804 805

C

Copy and complete the calculation squares.

1.

+	100	10	1000
598	698		
279			
935		945	
99			

2.

−	10	1	100
2510	2500		
1036			
5104		5103	
3800			

Count on in 100s.
3. 500 from 860
4. 600 from 1530
5. 700 from 439
6. 800 from 1748

Count back in 10s.
7. 40 from 1613
8. 50 from 1020
9. 60 from 829
10. 70 from 5046

Write the next three numbers in these sequences.
11. 996 997 998 999
12. 4030 4020 4010 4000
13. 1580 1680 1780 1880
14. 2385 2285 2185 2085
15. 1340 1330 1320 1310
16. 304 303 302 301

On this page you will learn to recognise odd and even numbers.

EVEN NUMBERS
Even numbers end in 0, 2, 4, 6 or 8.

ODD NUMBERS
Odd numbers end in 1, 3, 5, 7 or 9.

Examples

312   78

170   4   926

Examples

89   801

3   415   47

A

Copy the sequences and write the missing numbers.

1 2 4 6 ☐ ☐

2 3 5 7 ☐ ☐

3 16 18 20 ☐ ☐

4 30 32 34 ☐ ☐

5 16 18 20 ☐ ☐

6 29 31 33 ☐ ☐

B

| 5 | 4 | 9 | 16 | 28 | 37 |
| 42 | 51 | 60 | 73 | 89 | 94 |

1 Which of these numbers are odd?

2 Which of these numbers are even?

3 2 and 4 are even numbers.
$2 + 4 = 6$ 6 is also an even number.
Try adding other even numbers. Is the answer always even?

C

| 34 | 106 | 93 | 210 | 185 | 77 |
| 362 | 41 | 128 | 299 | 453 | 504 |

1 Give the next odd number after all of the above numbers.

2 Give the next even number after all of the above numbers.

3 3 and 5 are odd numbers.
$3 + 5 = 8$ 8 is an even number.
Try adding other odd numbers. Is the answer always even?

4 What happens if you add an odd number and an even number?

On this page you will learn to extend number sequences.

To find the rule that links the numbers look at the gaps.

Examples

2 4 6 8 10   The rule is 'add 2'.

20 16 12 8 4   The rule is 'subtract 4'.

A

Copy and complete by filling in the boxes.

1. 16 18 20 22 □ □
2. 9 12 15 18 □ □
3. 12 16 20 24 □ □
4. 5 10 15 20 □ □
5. 29 31 33 35 □ □
6. 22 18 14 10 □ □

7. 17 22 27 32 □ □
8. 4 7 10 13 □ □
9. 17 15 13 11 □ □
10. 28 23 18 13 □ □
11. 3 7 11 15 □ □
12. 24 21 18 15 □ □

B

Copy the sequences and write the next three numbers.
What is the rule for each sequence?

1. 17 19 21 23
2. 30 34 38 42
3. 9 14 19 24
4. 937 837 737 637

5. 51 49 47 45
6. 16 26 36 46
7. 52 47 42 37
8. 63 66 69 72

9. 84 74 64 54
10. 97 93 89 85
11. 143 243 343 543
12. 58 55 52 49

C

Write the first six numbers in each sequence.

	Start at	Rule		Start at	Rule
1	19	Add 3	7	20	Add 30
2	180	Subtract 20	8	70	Subtract 7
3	12	Add 6	9	70	Add 40
4	72	Subtract 9	10	30	Subtract 4
5	40	Add 8	11	25	Add 25
6	86	Subtract 11	12	325	Subtract 50

On this page you will learn to recognise multiples.

Multiples are the numbers in a multiplication table.

Examples
The multiples of 2 are 2, 4, 6, 8, 10, 12, etc.
The multiples of 3 are 3, 6, 9, 12, 15, 18, etc.

A

Write the first four multiples of:

1 2   **3** 10

2 3   **4** 5.

Write down the numbers in the ring which are multiples of:

5 10   **7** 3

6 2   **8** 5.

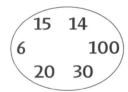

9 Is 18 a multiple of 3?

10 Is 21 a multiple of 2?

11 Is 35 a multiple of 5?

12 Is 18 a multiple of 4?

13 Is 55 a multiple of 10?

14 Is 14 a multiple of 2?

15 Is 23 a multiple of 3?

16 Is 24 a multiple of 4?

B

Write the first four multiples of:

1 50   **3** 100

2 4   **4** 6.

Write down the numbers in the ring which are multiples of:

5 2   **7** 5

6 50   **8** 10.

100   75
52   200
55   150

Copy and complete the sentences.

9 The multiples of 2 are ☐ numbers.

10 The multiples of 5 end in ☐ or ☐.

11 The multiples of 10 end in ☐.

12 The multiples of ☐ end in 50 or 00.

13 The multiples of ☐ end in 00.

C

Which number should not be in the box?

1 | Multiples of 2
12, 8, 9, 18

2 | Multiples of 5
15, 10, 12, 25

3 | Multiples of 3
9, 10, 15, 24

4 | Multiples of 4
14, 16, 20, 32

5 10 is a multiple of 2 and a multiple of 5.
Find another number that is a multiple of both 2 and 5.

6 Find two numbers that are multiples of both:
a) 2 and 3
b) 3 and 4
c) 3 and 5
d) 5 and 10.
e) 4 and 5.

On this page you will learn to know what each digit in a number represents and how to partition (break up) a number.

Examples

369   The 3 has a value of 300.   517   The 5 has a value of 500.
         The 6 has a value of 60.   The 1 has a value of 10.
         The 9 has a value of 9 units.   The 7 has a value of 7 units.

Knowing the value of the digits means that you are able to partition numbers.

Examples

$369 = 300 + 60 + 9$ $517 = 500 + 10 + 7$

A

Copy and complete by filling in the boxes.

1. $26 = 20 + \square$
2. $57 = 50 + \square$
3. $48 = \square + 8$
4. $63 = \square + 3$
5. $\square = 70 + 1$
6. $\square = 80 + 3$
7. $35 = 30 + \square$
8. $14 = 10 + \square$
9. $72 = \square + 2$
10. $15 = \square + 5$
11. $\square = 30 + 7$
12. $\square = 20 + 4$
13. $43 = 40 + \square$
14. $92 = 90 + \square$
15. $34 = \square + 4$
16. $91 = \square + 1$
17. $\square = 40 + 8$
18. $\square = 70 + 6$

B

What is the value of the digit underlined?

1. 1<u>3</u>6
2. <u>2</u>40
3. 38<u>5</u>
4. <u>1</u>64
5. 51<u>2</u>
6. 8<u>7</u>9
7. 75<u>8</u>
8. 4<u>9</u>3
9. <u>6</u>21
10. 90<u>6</u>
11. <u>3</u>24
12. 5<u>8</u>7

Partition these numbers as in the example.

13. 497
14. 613
15. 154
16. 582
17. 731
18. 240
19. 925
20. 382
21. 601
22. 476
23. 859
24. 648
25. 354
26. 206
27. 915
28. 837
29. 671
30. 428

C

What is the value of the digit underlined?

1. 4<u>8</u>62
2. 135<u>4</u>
3. <u>2</u>739
4. 1<u>5</u>76
5. <u>3</u>190
6. <u>8</u>627
7. 548<u>3</u>
8. 7<u>9</u>01
9. 38<u>1</u>0
10. 624<u>8</u>
11. <u>4</u>063
12. 91<u>7</u>8

Work out:

13. $1942 + 30$
14. $3402 + 500$
15. $3485 + 2000$
16. $6856 + 70$
17. $4327 + 4000$
18. $8514 + 600$
19. $1683 + 60$
20. $7061 + 2000$
21. $4735 + 700$
22. $6912 + 3000$
23. $6359 + 90$
24. $5726 + 800.$

On these pages you will learn:

• to order a set of numbers in order of size.

Compare the highest value digits (the digit on the left).

Example

561   651   647

Put these numbers in order with the smallest first.
Look at the hundreds first.

561   651   647
↓   ↓   ↓
500   600   600

If the hundreds are the same, look at the tens.

651   647
↓   ↓
50   40

The correct order is 561, 647, 651

• to work out the number lying half-way between two other numbers.

Example

Find the number lying halfway between 30 and 40.
a) Find the difference between the numbers.
b) Work out half the difference.
c) Add half the difference to the lower number.

a) $40 - 30 = 10$
b) $10 \div 2 = 5$
c) $30 + 5 = 35$

35 is half way between 30 and 40.

A

Starting with Sunday, write down which day of the week is:
1 second   4 third
2 fifth   5 sixth
3 last   6 fourth.

Which number is smaller?
7 27 or 72   10 63 or 36
8 57 or 75   11 43 or 34
9 76 or 67   12 89 or 98

Which number is larger?
13 83 or 38   16 52 or 25
14 68 or 86   17 45 or 54
15 73 or 37   18 87 or 78

Copy and complete by filling in any numbers in the boxes so that the numbers are in order.
19 ☐ 48 ☐ 50 51

20 ☐ 36 ☐ 42 47

21 66 67 ☐ ☐ 70

22 74 ☐ 82 ☐ 90

Find the number that is halfway on each of these number lines.
23 10 ——————————|—————————— 20

24 11 ——————————|—————————— 15

B

Which month of the year is:
1. first
2. eighth
3. last
4. third
5. tenth
6. sixth?

Which number is smaller?
7. 372 or 327
8. 264 or 246
9. 534 or 543
10. 514 or 541
11. 756 or 765
12. 687 or 678

Which number is larger?
13. 239 or 293
14. 342 or 324
15. 598 or 589
16. 485 or 458
17. 745 or 754
18. 612 or 621

Put these sets of numbers in order, starting with the smallest.
19. 174 253 273 147
20. 583 495 538 459
21. 412 396 369 421 391
22. 714 682 741 671 628

Find the number that is halfway on each of these number lines.
23. 30 ———— 40
24. 200 ———— 300
25. 40 ———— 60
26. 8 ———— 9
27. 55 ———— 65
28. 100 ———— 110

C

Here are some black and white beads.

● ○ ○ ● ○ ● ○ ○ ●

What colour are the following beads?
1. the 2nd
2. the 5th
3. the 7th
4. the last

If the pattern was continued what colour would these beads be?
5. the 15th
6. the 19th
7. the 28th
8. the 32nd

Work out the number that is halfway between:
9. 1000 and 2000
10. 1360 and 1380
11. 1940 and 2000
12. 3190 and 3210
13. 2540 and 2550
14. 4950 and 5050.

Put these numbers in order, starting with the smallest.
15. 6259 5962 6952 5682 6529
16. 3784 4738 3478 3874 4378
17. 1524 2145 1452 1245 2451
18. 8739 7938 8973 7839 8379
19. 5827 6234 6324 5782 6432
20. 5293 5932 4816 5329 4681
21. 6741 1476 6471 1674 1746
22. 9682 9268 8692 9862 8962

On these pages you will learn to add or subtract 1, 10 or 100 from a whole number.

To add 1 to a number add 1 to the digit in the units column.
To add 10 to a number add 1 to the digit in the tens column.
To add 100 to a number add 1 to the digit in the hundreds column.
Subtraction works in a similar way.

Examples

$357 + 1 = 358$ $357 - 1 = 356$
$357 + 10 = 367$ $357 - 10 = 347$
$357 + 100 = 457$ $357 - 100 = 257$

$129 + 1 = 130$ $250 - 1 = 249$
$190 + 10 = 200$ $400 - 10 = 390$
$900 + 100 = 1000$ $1057 - 100 = 957$

 A

What number is:

1 more than	1 less than	10 more than	10 less than
1 68	**5** 48	**9** 35	**13** 50
2 29	**6** 70	**10** 61	**14** 68
3 104	**7** 136	**11** 115	**15** 76
4 119	**8** 150	**12** 93	**16** 102

17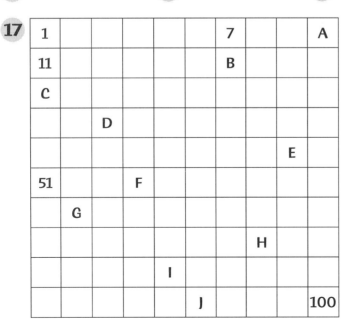

This is a 1 to 100 number square.

Only a few of the numbers are shown.

Write down each letter and the number that should be in that square.
Example A = 10

B

These are parts of the 1 to 100 square. Which numbers are shown by the letters?

1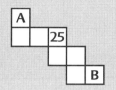

3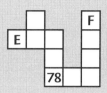

5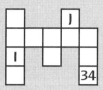

7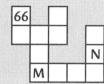

2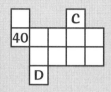

4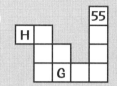

6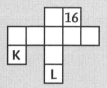

8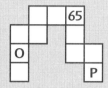

Copy and complete by filling in the box.

9 $217 \xrightarrow{+1} \square$

13 $158 \xrightarrow{-1} \square$

17 $441 \xrightarrow{+100} \square$

10 $\square \xrightarrow{+1} 378$

14 $\square \xrightarrow{+10} 803$

18 $\square \xrightarrow{+100} 214$

11 $135 \xrightarrow{-1} \square$

15 $529 \xrightarrow{-10} \square$

19 $682 \xrightarrow{-100} \square$

12 $\square \xrightarrow{-1} 463$

16 $\square \xrightarrow{+100} 397$

20 $\square \xrightarrow{-100} 35$

C

What number is:

100 more than	100 less than	1000 more than	1000 less than
1 1364	**5** 1573	**9** 2011	**13** 1637
2 2900	**6** 3058	**10** 3746	**14** 5200
3 6725	**7** 4892	**11** 7489	**15** 2574
4 3917	**8** 6020	**12** 9365	**16** 10 828.

Copy and complete by filling in the box.

17 $2596 \xrightarrow{+10} \square$

20 $\square \xrightarrow{+10} 1268$

23 $6801 \xrightarrow{-10} \square$

26 $\square \xrightarrow{-10} 9473$

18 $8439 \xrightarrow{+100} \square$

21 $\square \xrightarrow{+100} 2096$

24 $5068 \xrightarrow{-100} \square$

27 $\square \xrightarrow{-100} 6902$

19 $3264 \xrightarrow{+1000} \square$

22 $\square \xrightarrow{+1000} 4127$

25 $1945 \xrightarrow{-1000} \square$

28 $\square \xrightarrow{-1000} 7853$

On this page you will practise estimating the position of a point on a line.

Estimate the numbers shown by each of the arrows.

A

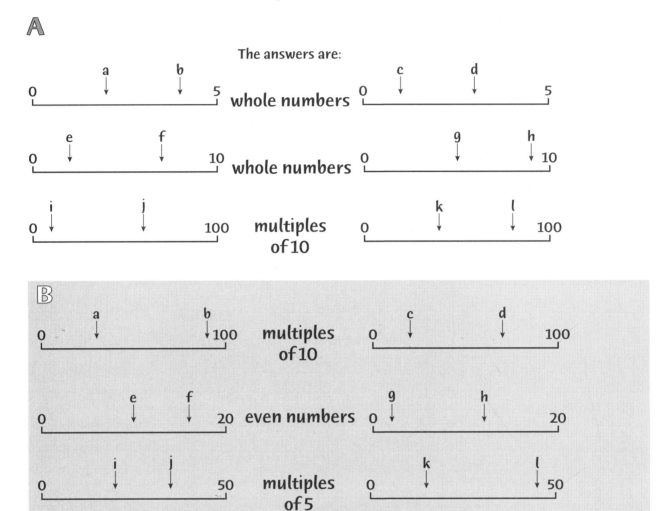

B

C

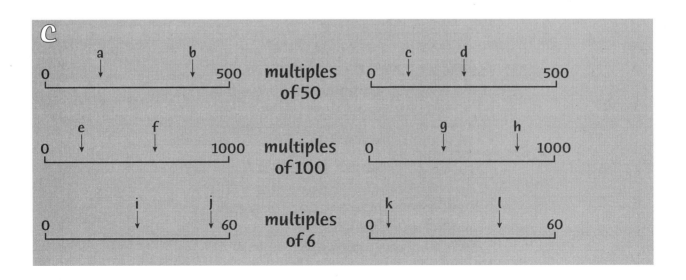

On this page you will learn to round a number to the nearest 10 or 100.

ROUNDING TO THE NEAREST 10	ROUNDING TO THE NEAREST 100
Look at the units column.	Look at the tens and units columns.
5 or more, round up.	50 or more, round up.
Less than 5, round down.	Less than 50, round down.
Examples	**Examples**
39 rounds to 40	462 rounds to 500
34 rounds to 30	448 rounds to 400
45 rounds to 50	750 rounds to 800

A

Copy and complete by rounding to the nearest 10.

1 23 rounds to ☐   **5** 44 rounds to ☐   **9** 31 rounds to ☐

2 78 rounds to ☐   **6** 35 rounds to ☐   **10** 58 rounds to ☐

3 92 rounds to ☐   **7** 87 rounds to ☐   **11** 43 rounds to ☐

4 16 rounds to ☐   **8** 69 rounds to ☐   **12** 46 rounds to ☐

B

Round to the nearest 10.   Round to the nearest 100.

1 84	**5** 13	**9** 17	**13** 130	**17** 620	**21** 952
2 37	**6** 25	**10** 33	**14** 460	**18** 850	**22** 495
3 29	**7** 61	**11** 65	**15** 380	**19** 573	**23** 847
4 72	**8** 48	**12** 98	**16** 710	**20** 208	**24** 796

C

Round to the nearest 10.   Round to the nearest 100.

1 168   **3** 289   **5** 103   **7** 382   **9** 756   **11** 1250   **13** 3582   **15** 2951

2 314   **4** 425   **6** 97   **8** 635   **10** 618   **12** 2815   **14** 1539   **16** 1497

Copy the sentences. Write the number to the nearest 1000 and use the word 'about'.

17 The shop sold 1750 cards in December.

18 The plane flew 3963 miles.

19 Amber has £5217 in the bank.

20 The encyclopaedia has 937 pages.

Merry Christmas

On these pages you will learn to recognise fractions.

A fraction is a number that is less than a whole one.
When a whole one is divided into equal parts each of the parts is a fraction of the whole one.

Examples

2 equal parts   4 equal parts   10 equal parts

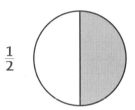   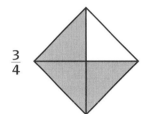   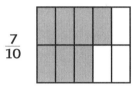

one half is shaded   three quarters is shaded   seven tenths is shaded

Write one half, one quarter or three quarters for each shape.
Write your answers in both words and figures.

1   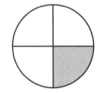   3   5   7

2   4   6   8

Copy and complete these sentences by writing the fractions in words.

9 [＿＿＿] of the shapes are circles.

10 [＿＿＿] of the shapes are black.

11 [＿＿＿] of the shapes are triangles.

12 [＿＿＿] of the shapes are not squares.

13 [＿＿＿] of the shapes are black circles.

14 [＿＿＿] of the shapes are not white circles.

B

What fraction of each diagram is shaded?
Write your answer in both words and figures.

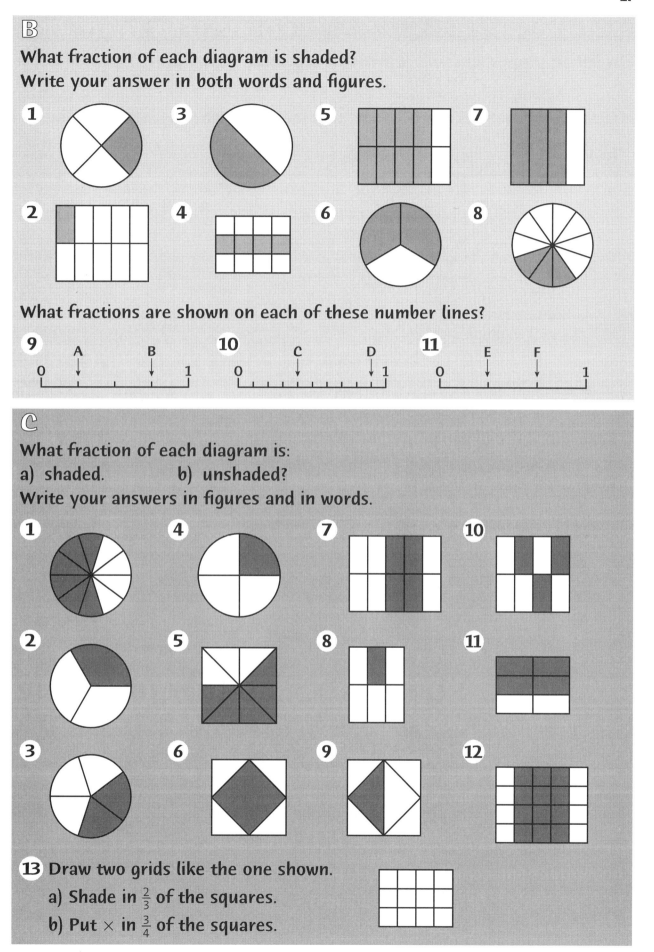

What fractions are shown on each of these number lines?

C

What fraction of each diagram is:
a) shaded.   b) unshaded?
Write your answers in figures and in words.

13 Draw two grids like the one shown.
   a) Shade in $\frac{2}{3}$ of the squares.
   b) Put × in $\frac{3}{4}$ of the squares.

On these pages you will learn to recognise equivalent fractions.

Equivalent fractions are fractions that look different but are the same.

Examples

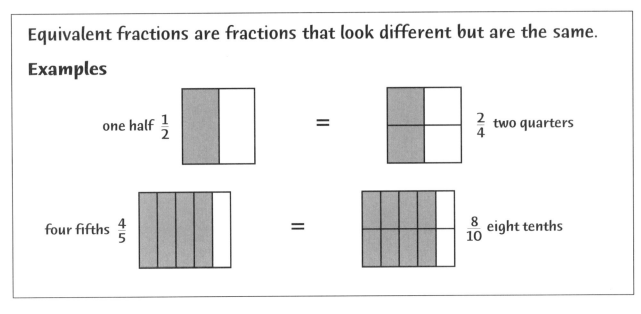

one half $\frac{1}{2}$ = $\frac{2}{4}$ two quarters

four fifths $\frac{4}{5}$ = $\frac{8}{10}$ eight tenths

A

Use a plain piece of paper.

Draw 3 rectangles by drawing round a template. (The rectangles must be exactly the same.)

Cut out the rectangles.

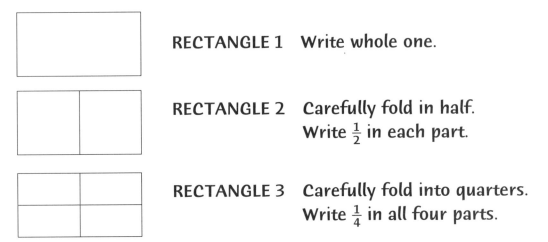

RECTANGLE 1   Write whole one.

RECTANGLE 2   Carefully fold in half.
Write $\frac{1}{2}$ in each part.

RECTANGLE 3   Carefully fold into quarters.
Write $\frac{1}{4}$ in all four parts.

Use your shapes to copy and complete the sentences.

1 One whole one equals ☐ halves.

2 One whole one equals ☐ quarters.

3 One half equals ☐ quarters.

B

whole		1
half		$\frac{1}{2}$
quarter		$\frac{1}{4}$
eigth		$\frac{1}{8}$

1		whole
$\frac{1}{2}$		half
$\frac{1}{5}$		fifth
$\frac{1}{10}$		tenth

Use the fraction charts to copy and complete by filling in the box.

1 $\frac{1}{2} = \frac{\square}{4}$

2 $1 = \frac{\square}{8}$

3 $\frac{1}{5} = \frac{\square}{10}$

4 $1 = \frac{\square}{5}$

5 $\frac{3}{4} = \frac{\square}{8}$

6 $\frac{1}{2} = \frac{\square}{10}$

7 $1 = \frac{\square}{4}$

8 $\frac{1}{4} = \frac{\square}{8}$

9 $1 = \frac{\square}{2}$

10 $\frac{3}{5} = \frac{\square}{10}$

11 $\frac{1}{2} = \frac{\square}{8}$

12 $1 = \frac{\square}{10}$

Copy and complete these fraction chains.

13 $\frac{1}{2} = \frac{\square}{4} = \frac{\square}{8} = \frac{\square}{16}$

14 $\frac{1}{2} = \frac{\square}{4} = \frac{\square}{6} = \frac{\square}{8} = \frac{\square}{10}$

C

Use squared paper.
Draw a fraction chart to show a whole one, thirds, sixths and twelfths.
Use your chart to complete these equivalent fractions.

1 $\frac{1}{2} = \frac{\square}{6}$

2 $\frac{1}{3} = \frac{\square}{6}$

3 $\frac{1}{6} = \frac{\square}{12}$

4 $\frac{2}{3} = \frac{\square}{6}$

5 $\frac{5}{6} = \frac{\square}{12}$

6 $1 = \frac{\square}{6}$

7 $\frac{1}{3} = \frac{\square}{12}$

8 $\frac{4}{6} = \frac{\square}{12}$

9 $\frac{1}{2} = \frac{\square}{12}$

10 $1 = \frac{\square}{12}$

11 $\frac{2}{3} = \frac{\square}{12}$

12 $\frac{2}{6} = \frac{\square}{12}$

Which is the odd one out in each set of fractions?

13 $\left(\frac{3}{7} \quad \frac{2}{4} \quad \frac{1}{2} \quad \frac{4}{8} \quad \frac{5}{10} \right)$

14 $\left(\frac{1}{5} \quad \frac{2}{10} \quad \frac{10}{50} \quad \frac{5}{20} \quad \frac{3}{15} \right)$

15 $\left(\frac{10}{15} \quad \frac{3}{6} \quad \frac{2}{3} \quad \frac{8}{12} \quad \frac{6}{9} \right)$

16 $\left(\frac{2}{8} \quad \frac{10}{40} \quad \frac{8}{16} \quad \frac{3}{12} \quad \frac{1}{4} \right)$

On this page you will learn to find fractions of quantities or numbers.

Examples

One half of 12p $12p \div 2 = 6p$ One tenth of 40p $40p \div 10 = 4p$

One quarter of 12p $12p \div 4 = 3p$ One eighth of 40p $40p \div 8 = 5p$

A

One half of $12 = 6$

One quarter of $12 = 3$

Use counters to find one half of:

1. 8 counters
2. 10 counters
3. 16 counters
4. 6 counters
5. 14 counters
6. 20 counters
7. 24 counters
8. 18 counters.

Find one quarter of:

9. 8 counters
10. 20 counters
11. 16 counters
12. 24 counters
13. 4 counters
14. 32 counters
15. 12 counters
16. 28 counters

B

Find one half of:

1. 16
2. 30
3. 26
4. 22
5. 14
6. 28.

Find one quarter of:

7. 20 cm
8. 40 cm
9. 36 cm
10. 24 cm
11. 28 cm
12. 32 cm.

Find one tenth of:

13. 10p
14. 50p
15. 20p
16. £1
17. 40p
18. 70p.

19. Jay has 16 sweets. He eats one quarter of them. How many sweets does he have left?

20. Alice has 24 books. Three quarters of them are stories. How many of her books are non-fiction?

C

Find

1. $\frac{1}{2}$ of 100
2. $\frac{1}{3}$ of 21
3. $\frac{1}{5}$ of 30
4. $\frac{1}{8}$ of 16
5. $\frac{1}{3}$ of 27
6. $\frac{1}{4}$ of 44
7. $\frac{1}{6}$ of 24
8. $\frac{1}{5}$ of 45
9. $\frac{1}{10}$ of 150
10. $\frac{1}{7}$ of 35
11. $\frac{1}{3}$ of 18
12. $\frac{1}{9}$ of 90.

What fraction of 20 is:

13. 10
15. 2
14. 5
16. 15?

What fraction of £1 is:

17. 10p
19. 50p
18. 75p
20. 20p?

What fraction of 30 cm is:

21. 10 cm
23. 6 cm
22. 15 cm
24. 20 cm?

On this page you will practise using addition facts.

A

Copy and complete the number pairs for 7.

1. $0 + \square = 7$
   $1 + \square = 7$
   $2 + \square = 7$
   $3 + \square = 7$
   $4 + \square = 7$
   $5 + \square = 7$
   $6 + \square = 7$
   $7 + \square = 7$

2. Write out the number pairs for:
   a) 6
   b) 8
   c) 9
   d) 10.

Find 4 pairs of numbers which make each target number.

3.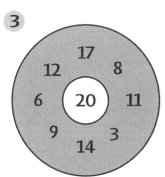

4.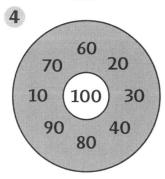

B

Work out:

1. $7 + 8$
2. $5 + 8$
3. $8 + 9$
4. $6 + 6$
5. $9 + 7$
6. $10 + 8$
7. $8 + 6$
8. $9 + 9$
9. $6 + 9$
10. $7 + 9$
11. $6 + 8$
12. $5 + 9$
13. $8 + 8$
14. $7 + 7$
15. $9 + 9$
16. $9 + 8.$

Take one number from each box. Find all six sums.

17. Example:
    $5 + 95 = 100$

5	35
85	75
65	45
45	95
25	15
55	55

$\square + \square = 100$

17.

400	800
600	900
100	600
700	500
500	300
200	400

$\square + \square = 1000$

C

Copy and complete.

1. $60 + \square = 120$
2. $70 + \square = 150$
3. $\square + 60 = 140$
4. $\square + 70 = 160$
5. $80 + \square = 180$
6. $80 + \square = 130$
7. $\square + 90 = 150$
8. $\square + 80 = 150$
9. $80 + \square = 160$
10. $90 + \square = 180$
11. $\square + 70 = 140$
12. $\square + 90 = 170$

What do you need to add to each number to make 100?

13. 28
14. 63
15. 39
16. 83
17. 19
18. 46
19. 68
20. 75
21. 34
22. 79
23. 41
24. 57

What do you need to add to each number to make 1000?

25. 850
26. 550
27. 150
28. 300
29. 750
30. 950
31. 250
32. 450
33. 700
34. 50
35. 350
36. 650

On these pages you will learn to understand the vocabulary and operation of addition.

- The order in which you add numbers does not change the answer.

Example A

$63 + 18 = 18 + 63 = 81$

Example B

$$15 + 17 + 3 = (15 + 17) + 3$$
$$= 32 + 3$$
$$= 35$$
$$15 + 17 + 3 = 15 + (17 + 3)$$
$$= 15 + 20$$
$$= 35$$

- Addition is the inverse of subtraction.

Example

Find the missing number.

$\square + 23 = 68$

The answer is 45 because
$68 - 23 = 45$.

Example

- Addition can be expressed in different ways.

Example

$47 + 29$

the sum of 47 and 29

add 47 to 29

47 add 69

the total of 47 and 29

47 and 29 altogether

47 plus 29

A

Work out:

1. The sum of 7 and 12.
2. 64 plus 11.
3. 400 add 300.
4. 72 and 7 altogether.
5. The total of 37 and 10.
6. Add 63 to 30.

7. 18 plus 7.
8. The sum of 43 and 14.
9. 30 add 23.
10. The total of 52 and 19.
11. Add 15 to 32.
12. 45 and 45 altogether.

Write true or false for each of these number sentences.

13. $7 + 14 = 14 + 7$
14. $32 + 6 = 23 + 6$
15. $2 + 3 + 4 = 4 + 3 + 2$
16. $3 + 4 = 4 + 5$
17. $2 + 7 + 4 = 2 + 4 + 7$
18. $600 + 8 = 800 + 6$

Copy and complete.

19. $6 + \square = 20$
20. $7 + \square = 16$
21. $\square + 40 = 100$
22. $\square + 8 = 25$
23. $40 + \square = 67$
24. $64 + \square = 77$

B

Copy and complete.

1. The total of 43 and 18 is ☐.
2. 70 plus ☐ equals 114.
3. ☐ add 25 equals 100.
4. The sum of 52 and ☐ is 79.
5. 16 and 16 altogether is ☐.
6. Add ☐ to 97 to make 107.
7. 74 plus 19 equals ☐.
8. ☐ add 400 equals 1000.
9. Add 61 to ☐ to make 361.
10. The total of 46 and 35 is ☐.
11. The sum of 21 and ☐ is 59.
12. ☐ and 400 altogether is 1200.

Find the totals. Work downwards. Check your answers by working upwards. Which way was easier?

13.
```
  16
   4
+  9
```

15.
```
   8
   9
+ 11
```

14.
```
   6
  17
+ 13
```

16.
```
  18
  12
+  7
```

Copy and complete.

17. $400 + ☐ = 458$
18. $90 + ☐ = 121$
19. $☐ + 19 = 84$
20. $☐ + 37 = 83$
21. $70 + ☐ = 130$
22. $75 + ☐ = 100$
23. $☐ + 25 = 58$
24. $☐ + 29 = 62$

C

Find the totals. Work from left to right.
Check your answers by working from right to left. Which way was easier?

1. $15 + 35 + 14$
2. $16 + 22 + 18$
3. $23 + 27 + 19$
4. $36 + 14 + 17$
5. $27 + 19 + 11$
6. $29 + 25 + 15$
7. $38 + 12 + 13$
8. $18 + 37 + 13$

Copy and complete.

9. $68 + ☐ = 100$
10. $160 + ☐ = 196$
11. $☐ + 16 = 300$
12. $☐ + 61 = 127$
13. $158 + ☐ = 165$
14. $232 + ☐ = 272$
15. $☐ + 49 = 124$
16. $☐ + 43 = 283$
17. $257 + ☐ = 300$
18. $76 + ☐ = 134$
19. $☐ + 800 = 2000$
20. $☐ + 37 = 100$

21. Write $48 + 35$ in words in six different ways.

22. A circus clown is fired 29 m on Monday and 36 m on Tuesday. How far is he fired altogether?

On these pages you will learn to understand the vocabulary and operation of subtraction.

TAKING AWAY

Examples

1. 7 take away 3.

2. 7 subtract 3.

FINDING A DIFFERENCE

Examples

1. What is the difference between 7 and 3?

2. How many more is 7 than 3?

3. How many less is 3 than 7?

THE INVERSE OF ADDITION

Examples

1. Find the missing number.

   $\square - 33 = 62.$

   The answer is 95 because
   $62 + 33 = 95.$

2. How many more must be added to 28 to make 37?

   The answer is 19 because
   $47 - 28 = 19.$

A

Work out:

1. Take 10 from 37.

2. 11 less than 54.

3. 104 subtract 5.

4. 20 less than 60.

5. 46 take away 8.

6. Subtract 7 from 22.

Copy and complete.

7. $65 - \square = 58$

8. $40 - \square = 33$

9. $\square - 9 = 38$

10. $\square - 5 = 27$

11. $21 - \square = 16$

12. $70 - \square = 40$

Find the difference between these numbers and the target number circled.

(24)	(65)
13 18	16 73
14 31	17 11
15 9	18 56.

How many more must be added to these numbers to make the target number?

(20)	(100)
19 8	22 20
20 13	23 70
21 6	24 50.

B

Work out:

1 Take 100 from 214.

2 21 less than 47.

3 502 subtract 8.

4 36 less than 89.

5 115 take away 40.

6 Subtract 6 from 74.

Copy and complete.

7 $400 - \square = 330$

8 $\square - 19 = 53$

9 $1002 - \square = 9$

10 $\square - 600 = 700$

11 $257 - \square = 247$

12 $\square - 45 = 100$

13 $743 - \square = 743$

14 $\square - 31 = 27$

Find the difference between these numbers and the target number circled.

⑲   ㊅⑻ (68)

15 28   18 77

16 43   19 42

17 75   20 94.

How many more must be added to these numbers to make the target number?

(100)   (1000)

21 45   24 800

22 25   25 100

23 65   26 700.

C

Find the difference between each pair of numbers.

1 178 31   5 230 160

2 6001 14   6 282 60

3 28   75   7 1700 800

4 254 69   8 83   57

How many more must be added to these numbers to make the target numbers?

(100)   (1000)

9 58   12 350

10 23   13 750

11 76   14 150.

15 Copy and complete the table showing children's marks in an end of year Maths Test.

Name	Paper A	Paper B	Total
Lee	47	46	93
Hayley	40		91
Craig	41		87
Lisa	39		82
Joanne	40		79
Tom	38		75
Stuart		39	74
Jodie		33	70
Carl		29	62
Lucy		28	56
Darren		25	53
Sharon		19	45

16 Write $57 - 23$ in words in as many ways as you can.

On this page you will practise using subtraction facts.

A

Write the answers only.

1 8 − 5   **9** 10 − 5

2 10 − 7   **10** 9 − 5

3 9 − 4   **11** 8 − 3

4 10 − 6   **12** 10 − 4

5 7 − 2   **13** 7 − 4

6 8 − 6   **14** 10 − 8

7 9 − 8   **15** 9 − 3

8 6 − 3   **16** 8 − 4

Take one number from each box. Make six subtractions.
Example 20 − 12 = 8

17

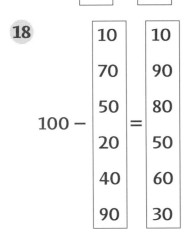

$$20 - \begin{array}{|c|} 12 \\ 5 \\ 9 \\ 16 \\ 13 \\ 6 \end{array} = \begin{array}{|c|} 4 \\ 15 \\ 11 \\ 14 \\ 7 \\ 8 \end{array}$$

18

$$100 - \begin{array}{|c|} 10 \\ 70 \\ 50 \\ 20 \\ 40 \\ 90 \end{array} = \begin{array}{|c|} 10 \\ 90 \\ 80 \\ 50 \\ 60 \\ 30 \end{array}$$

B

Write the answers only.

1 20 − 8   **9** 19 − 7

2 18 − 11   **10** 18 − 9

3 17 − 8   **11** 16 − 7

4 19 − 12   **12** 17 − 6

5 15 − 8   **13** 20 − 9

6 16 − 9   **14** 19 − 14

7 14 − 6   **15** 18 − 5

8 20 − 13   **16** 17 − 9

Take one number from each box. Make six subtractions.
Example 100 − 15 = 85

17

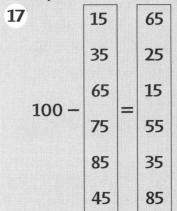

$$100 - \begin{array}{|c|} 15 \\ 35 \\ 65 \\ 75 \\ 85 \\ 45 \end{array} = \begin{array}{|c|} 65 \\ 25 \\ 15 \\ 55 \\ 35 \\ 85 \end{array}$$

18

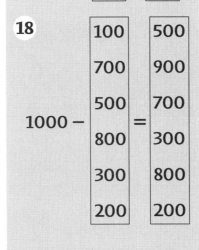

$$1000 - \begin{array}{|c|} 100 \\ 700 \\ 500 \\ 800 \\ 300 \\ 200 \end{array} = \begin{array}{|c|} 500 \\ 900 \\ 700 \\ 300 \\ 800 \\ 200 \end{array}$$

C

Copy and complete.

1 200 − ☐ = 110

2 150 − ☐ = 80

3 ☐ − 90 = 90

4 ☐ − 70 = 90

5 190 − ☐ = 80

6 180 − ☐ = 130

7 ☐ − 70 = 130

8 ☐ − 80 = 90

9 160 − ☐ = 90

10 200 − ☐ = 60

11 ☐ − 80 = 110

12 ☐ − 60 = 120

Find the difference between each number in the outer ring and the target number.

17

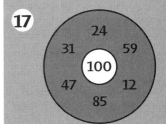

18

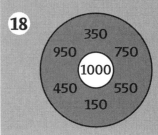

On this page you will learn to partition and recombine.

Break 6, 7, 8, 9 into '5 and a bit'.

Example

$$39 + 18 = (35 + 4) + (15 + 3)$$
$$= (35 + 15) + (4 + 3)$$
$$= 50 + 7 = 57$$

Partition into 10s and units.

Example

$$37 + 26 = (30 + 7) + (20 + 6)$$
$$= (30 + 20) + (7 + 6)$$
$$= 50 + 13 = 63$$

A

Work out:

1. $6 + 7$
2. $9 + 8$
3. $7 + 8$
4. $9 + 6$
5. $12 + 26$
6. $15 + 29$
7. $16 + 15$
8. $13 + 38$.

B

Work out by partitioning.

1. $25 + 18$
2. $45 + 17$
3. $35 + 29$
4. $65 + 18$
5. $55 + 39$
6. $45 + 28$
7. $75 + 19$
8. $25 + 27$
9. $55 + 46$
10. $65 + 26$
11. $28 + 37$
12. $47 + 22$
13. $35 + 43$
14. $52 + 36$
15. $74 + 23$
16. $61 + 27$

C

Work out by partitioning.

1. $34 + 19$
2. $45 + 38$
3. $67 + 24$
4. $58 + 29$
5. $36 + 87$
6. $52 + 49$
7. $43 + 76$
8. $64 + 58$
9. $58 − 14$
10. $74 − 23$
11. $86 − 41$
12. $67 − 35$
13. $49 − 27$
14. $89 − 25$
15. $78 − 56$
16. $57 − 42$

Now you will learn to use the relationship between addition and subtraction.

Knowing one + or − fact means that you know 3 other facts.

Example
$$28 + 16 = 44 \qquad 16 + 28 = 44$$
$$44 − 28 = 16 \qquad 44 − 16 = 28$$

A

Copy and complete using the 3 given numbers only.

 1. $8 + 6 = 14$

$\square + \square = 14$
$\square − \square = 8$
$\square − \square = 6$

2. $23 − 7 = 16$

$\square − \square = 7$
$\square + \square = 23$
$\square + \square = 23$

B

Copy and complete using the 3 given numbers only.

1. $48 + 37 = 85$

$\square + \square = 85$
$\square − \square = 48$
$\square − \square = 37$

3. $53 + 21 = 74$

$\square + \square = 74$
$\square − \square = 21$
$\square − \square = 53$

2. $68 − 35 = 33$

$\square − \square = 35$
$\square + \square = 68$
$\square + \square = 68$

4. $92 − 63 = 29$

$\square − \square = 63$
$\square + \square = 92$
$\square + \square = 92$

C

For each fact write 3 other facts.

1. $33 + 17 = 40$
2. $52 − 28 = 24$
3. $67 + 26 = 93$
4. $75 − 17 = 58$
5. $46 + 25 = 71$
6. $63 − 34 = 29$
7. $54 + 28 = 82$
8. $80 − 44 = 36$

On this page you will learn to add or subtract 9, 11, 19 . . . or 11, 21, 31 . . .

Examples

$64 + 19 = 64 + 20 - 1$
$\qquad = 84 - 1$
$\qquad = 83$

$55 + 31 = 55 + 30 + 1$
$\qquad = 85 + 1$
$\qquad = 86$

$48 - 19 = 48 - 20 + 1$
$\qquad = 28 + 1$
$\qquad = 29$

A

Copy and complete the patterns.

1. Add 9 $\boxed{7}$ $\boxed{}$ $\boxed{}$ $\boxed{34}$
2. Add 11 $\boxed{31}$ $\boxed{}$ $\boxed{}$ $\boxed{64}$
3. Add 19 $\boxed{8}$ $\boxed{}$ $\boxed{}$ $\boxed{65}$
4. Add 21 $\boxed{12}$ $\boxed{}$ $\boxed{}$ $\boxed{75}$
5. Take 9 $\boxed{51}$ $\boxed{}$ $\boxed{}$ $\boxed{24}$
6. Take 11 $\boxed{48}$ $\boxed{}$ $\boxed{}$ $\boxed{15}$
7. Take 19 $\boxed{96}$ $\boxed{}$ $\boxed{}$ $\boxed{39}$
8. Take 21 $\boxed{89}$ $\boxed{}$ $\boxed{}$ $\boxed{26}$

B

Add 11	Add 29
1 121	9 37
2 304	10 54
3 265	11 23
4 547	12 69

Take 9	Take 21
5 380	13 72
6 167	14 45
7 431	15 26
8 275	16 58

C

Copy and complete.

1. $\square + 21 = 35$
2. $\square + 41 = 98$
3. $\square + 31 = 124$
4. $\square + 61 = 149$
5. $\square - 31 = 42$
6. $\square - 61 = 27$
7. $\square - 51 = 83$
8. $\square - 81 = 76$

Now you will learn to use near doubles to add or subtract.

Examples

$35 + 37 = 35 + 35 + 2 = \text{Double } 35 + 2 = 70 + 2 = 72$
$18 + 16 = 18 + 18 - 2 = \text{Double } 18 - 2 = 36 - 2 = 34$

A

Work out:

1. $6 + 7$
2. $12 + 13$
3. $8 + 7$
4. $14 + 13$
5. $30 + 29$
6. $8 + 9$
7. $11 + 12$
8. $40 + 41.$

B

Work out:

1. $25 + 26$
2. $16 + 18$
3. $70 + 80$
4. $55 + 53$
5. $90 + 80$
6. $35 + 34$
7. $60 + 70$
8. $18 + 20$
9. $16 + 14$
10. $80 + 70$
11. $65 + 66$
12. $19 + 17$
13. $80 + 90$
14. $85 + 87$
15. $17 + 18$
16. $75 + 74.$

C

Work out:

1. $460 + 460$
2. $290 + 290$
3. $370 + 370$
4. $480 + 480$
5. $390 + 390$
6. $280 + 280$
7. $360 + 360$
8. $470 + 470.$

On this page you will learn to develop a pattern.

Example 1

$13 + 5 = 18$
$13 + 15 = 28$
$13 + 25 = 38$
and so on

Example 2

$4 + 8 = 12$
$40 + 80 = 120$
$400 + 800 = 1200$

Example 3

+	2	4	6	8
1	3	5	7	9
2	4	6	8	10
3	5	7	9	11
4	6	8	10	12

PATTERNS

Down   'Add 1'
Across   'Add 2'
Diagonal ↗ 'Add 1'
Diagonal ↘ 'Add 3'

A

Continue the pattern from:

1 $3 + 4 = 7$
$13 + 4 = 17$
to
$93 + 4 = 97$

2 $9 - 5 = 4$
$19 - 5 = 14$
to
$99 - 5 = 94.$

Copy and complete as in Example 2.

3 $5 + 3 = 8$
$50 + \square = \square$
$500 + \square = \square$

4 $8 - 6 = 2$
$\square - \square = \square$
$\square - \square = \square$

B

Continue the pattern from:

1 $12 + 7 = 19$
to
$12 + 97 = 109$

2 $99 - 4 = 95$
to
$99 - 94 = 5.$

Develop a pattern as in Example 2.

3 $6 + 7 = 13$

4 $15 - 8 = 7$

5 Copy and complete. Describe the patterns.

+	1	3	5	7
2				
4				
6				
8				

C

Copy and complete. Extend each square into an 8 × 8 grid.

1

+	3	6	9
2			
4			
6			

2

+	3	7	11
1			
3			
5			

3

+	2	4	6
5			
10			
15			

4

+	4	8	12
1			
4			
7			

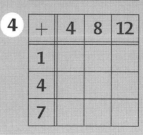

On this page you will practise adding or subtracting single digit or two-digit numbers.

A

Copy and complete the squares.

1

+	6	4	7
50			
42			
200			

2

+	5	3	8
61			
30			
500			

3

−	6	3	4
48			
70			
67			

4

+	15	13	16
22			
31			
43			

5

−	14	12	15
38			
59			
76			

B

Write the answers only.

1 $163 + 3$
2 $411 + 7$
3 $189 + 1$
4 $234 + 5$
5 $340 + 2$

6 $318 − 5$
7 $487 − 6$
8 $629 − 7$
9 $156 − 3$
10 $600 − 8$

Add 36
11 200
12 90
13 43.

Add 52
20 300
21 80
22 26.

Add 23
14 200
15 90
16 43.

Add 24
23 75
24 48
25 37.

Add 44
17 500
18 70
19 31.

Add 35
26 68
27 96
28 89.

29

27 people left a crowd of 89 people. How many people were now in the crowd?

C

Copy and complete.

1 $218 + \square = 225$
2 $677 + \square = 681$
3 $\square + 9 = 344$
4 $\square + 6 = 462$

5 $45 + \square = 73$
6 $69 + \square = 92$
7 $\square + 34 = 71$
8 $\square + 28 = 54$

9 $82 − \square = 58$
10 $64 − \square = 27$
11 $\square − 68 = 25$
12 $\square − 46 = 49$

13 $286 − \square = 278$
14 $715 − \square = 709$
15 $\square − 5 = 367$
16 $\square − 8 = 445$

17 $1000 − \square = 996$
18 $3000 − \square = 2993$
19 $\square − 2 = 1998$
20 $\square − 9 = 5991$

21 $1651 − \square = 1646$
22 $5136 − \square = 5129$
23 $\square − 6 = 3837$
24 $\square − 4 = 9068.$

On this page you will practise adding or subtracting multiples of 10 and 100.

A

Write the answers only.

1. 23 + 10
2. 40 + 30
3. 62 + 50
4. 400 + 200
5. 38 + 10
6. 30 + 50
7. 57 + 40
8. 600 + 300
9. 45 + 10
10. 20 + 40
11. 63 + 30
12. 500 + 100
13. 72 − 10
14. 90 − 30
15. 85 − 50
16. 800 − 400
17. 50 − 10
18. 81 − 50
19. 59 − 40
20. 700 − 500
21. 60 − 40
22. 100 − 10
23. 900 − 400
24. 76 − 30.

B

Add 10	Take 80
1 327	13 155
2 99	14 140
3 464	15 126
4 195.	16 130.

Take 10	Add 90
5 142	17 60
6 208	18 38
7 576	19 80
8 603.	20 23.

Add 60	Take 70
9 40	21 119
10 81	22 160
11 70	23 132
12 67.	24 120.

Copy and complete:

25. 170 + ☐ = 200
26. 456 + ☐ = 556
27. 325 − ☐ = 225
28. 340 + ☐ = 400
29. 283 + ☐ = 383
30. 749 − ☐ = 649
31. 400 + ☐ = 1100
32. 290 + ☐ = 300
33. 1200 − ☐ = 400
34. 520 + ☐ = 600
35. 800 + ☐ = 1300
36. 1600 − ☐ = 700.

C

Add 60	Take 70
1 278	13 435
2 381	14 629
3 455	15 712
4 763.	16 556.

Add 70	Take 80
5 294	17 367
6 546	18 943
7 482	19 779
8 679.	20 434.

Add 80	Take 90
9 357	21 251
10 894	22 886
11 238	23 622
12 561.	24 548.

Copy and complete.

25. 247 + ☐ = 300
26. 1600 + ☐ = 2000
27. 336 + ☐ = 400
28. 3200 + ☐ = 4000
29. 472 + ☐ = 500
30. 2300 + ☐ = 3000
31. 753 + ☐ = 800
32. 5400 + ☐ = 6000
33. 584 + ☐ = 600
34. 7800 + ☐ = 8000
35. 818 + ☐ = 900
36. 8100 + ☐ = 9000.

On this page you will learn:

● to add or subtract by bridging.

Examples

$67 + 9 = 67 + 3 + 6$
$\qquad = 70 + 6$
$\qquad = 76$

$54 - 7 = 54 - 4 - 3$
$\qquad = 50 - 3$
$\qquad = 47$

$64 - 35 = 64 - 30 - 5$
$\qquad = 34 - 5$
$\qquad = 29$

● to find a small difference by counting up.

Examples

$403 - 396 = 4 + 3$
$\qquad = 7$

$607 - 598 = 2 + 7$
$\qquad = 9$

$1005 - 993 = 7 + 5$
$\qquad = 12$

A

Add 7	Take 8
1 9	**7** 14
2 17	**8** 25
3 5	**9** 17
4 14	**10** 21
5 8	**11** 12
6 19	**12** 23

Find:

13 8 less than 23

14 27 less than 36

15 45 less than 52

16 68 less than 74

17 87 less than 91

18 95 less than 103

19 34 less than 42

20 56 less than 65

21 48 less than 56.

B

Work out:

1 $25 + 8$

2 $27 + 6$

3 $38 + 5$

4 $54 + 7$

5 $35 - 8$

6 $14 - 7$

7 $16 - 8$

8 $22 - 6$

9 $505 - 499$

10 $604 - 598$

11 $202 - 197$

12 $304 - 296$

13 $706 - 698$

14 $405 - 396$

15 $603 - 598$

16 $501 - 493.$

C

Copy and complete:

1 $46 + \square = 73$

2 $35 + \square = 83$

3 $63 - \square = 28$

4 $84 - \square = 28$

5 $\square + 22 = 81$

6 $\square + 49 = 93$

7 $\square - 28 = 33$

8 $\square - 36 = 57$

9 $1005 - \square = 7$

10 $2007 - \square = 13$

11 $4002 - \square = 14$

12 $8006 - \square = 17$

13 $\square - 2993 = 16$

14 $\square - 3991 = 15$

15 $\square - 1983 = 18$

16 $\square - 5985 = 19.$

A

There are 4 ways of making 11 by adding three odd numbers.

$1+1+9$ $1+5+5$
$1+3+7$ $3+3+5$

1 Find 5 ways of making 13 by adding 3 odd numbers.

2 Find 7 ways of making 15 by adding 3 odd numbers.

3 Find 4 ways of making 14 by adding 3 even numbers.

4 Find 5 ways of making 16 by adding 3 even numbers.

B

1 Find 6 ways of making 14 by adding 4 odd numbers.

2 Find 8 ways of making 16 by adding 4 odd numbers.

Find the missing digits.

3 $23 + \square 2 = 45$

4 $26 + 2\square = 49$

5 $16 + \square 7 = 33$

6 $2\square + 15 = 40$

7 $\square 3 + 1\square = 38$

8 $\square 8 + 14 = 32$

9 $3\square + \square 0 = 55$

10 $26 + 1\square = 45$

11 $39 - \square 1 = 8$

12 $2\square - 15 = 12$

13 $\square 2 - 1\square = 40$

14 $3\square - 14 = 18$

C

Find the missing digits.

1 $\square 6 + 24 = 60$

2 $7\square + \square 2 = 118$

3 $58 + 3\square = 97$

4 $8\square + 28 = 111$

5 $46 - 1\square = 29$

6 $6\square - \square 3 = 46$

7 $\square 5 - 2\square = 24$

8 $4\square - \square 6 = 12$

9 $1\square \times 6 = 84$

10 $\square 7 \times 5 = 135$

11 $2\square \times 4 = 92$

12 $\square 3 \times 3 = 159$

Copy and complete the sums.

13
$$\begin{array}{r} 4\square \\ + \square 6 \\ \hline 6\ 9 \end{array}$$

14
$$\begin{array}{r} \square 2 \\ + 2\square \\ \hline 5\ 7 \end{array}$$

15
$$\begin{array}{r} 5\square \\ + \square 4 \\ \hline 8\ 9 \end{array}$$

16
$$\begin{array}{r} \square 2 \\ + 2\square \\ \hline 8\ 8 \end{array}$$

17
$$\begin{array}{r} 4\square \\ + \square 4 \\ \hline 7\ 7 \end{array}$$

18
$$\begin{array}{r} \square 4 \\ + 2\square \\ \hline 8\ 1 \end{array}$$

19
$$\begin{array}{r} 3\square \\ + \square 3 \\ \hline 7\ 2 \end{array}$$

20
$$\begin{array}{r} \square 8 \\ + 1\square \\ \hline 8\ 4 \end{array}$$

On these pages you will learn to add several small numbers mentally.

● Look for pairs that make 10 or multiples of 10. Add these first.

Examples

$$7 + 9 + 2 + 8 = 7 + 9 + 10$$
$$= 16 + 10$$
$$= 26$$

$$8 + 6 + 13 + 7 = 8 + 6 + 20$$
$$= 14 + 20$$
$$= 34$$

● Start with the largest number.

Examples

$$9 + 12 + 17 + 6 = 9 + 12 + 23$$
$$= 9 + 35$$
$$= 44$$

$$5 + 7 + 4 + 22 = 5 + 7 + 26$$
$$= 12 + 26$$
$$= 38$$

 A

Find the totals.

1. $3 + 7 + 8$
2. $2 + 6 + 14$
3. $9 + 8 + 2$
4. $3 + 2 + 16$
5. $4 + 4 + 6$

6. $4 + 7 + 13$
7. $7 + 9 + 1$
8. $5 + 3 + 12$
9. $6 + 5 + 5$
10. $4 + 17 + 3$

11. $5 + 9 + 11$
12. $4 + 5 + 15$
13. $6 + 8 + 12$
14. $3 + 2 + 18$
15. $14 + 3 + 7$

3 darts can be thrown at this dartboard.

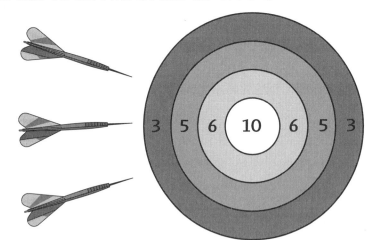

Examples

3, 3, 6 scores 12
5, 5, 5 scores 15
10, 3, 5 scores 18

Find ways of scoring:

16. 21
17. 11

18. 19
19. 14

20. 22
21. 16

22. 20
23. 13

24. 26
25. 17.

B

Copy and complete by filling in the box.

1 ☐ + 7 + 8 + 2 = 26

2 2 + ☐ + 7 + 3 = 27

3 18 + ☐ + 6 + 4 = 35

4 5 + ☐ + 16 + 5 = 30

5 19 + 8 + 11 + ☐ = 43

6 6 + 13 + ☐ + 7 = 34

7 2 + 3 + 18 + ☐ = 29

8 ☐ + 14 + 2 + 6 = 27

9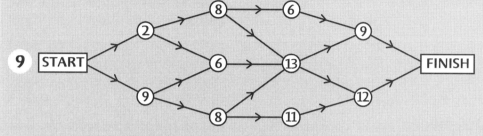

There are ten ways of going from the Start to the Finish.
Find the total for each of the ten ways.

C

Copy and complete by filling in the box.

1 6 + 8 + 4 + ☐ + 17 = 47

2 ☐ + 12 + 23 + 8 + 6 = 57

3 3 + 9 + 24 + 7 + ☐ = 50

4 9 + 16 + ☐ + 1 + 7 = 40

5 5 + ☐ + 4 + 18 + 5 = 37

6 26 + 8 + ☐ + 9 + 2 = 52

7 4 + ☐ + 19 + 6 + 7 = 48

8 6 + 7 + ☐ + 5 + 16 = 38

Use 3 darts.

Example

5, 5, 9 scores 19

Use 3 darts

9 What is the highest possible score?

10 What scores between 11 and 20 are possible?

11 What scores between 21 and 30 are not possible?

12 Four scores can be made in more than one way. What are they?

On this page you will learn to use jottings to support mental methods for addition.

Examples

$$78 + 45 = 78 + 40 + 5$$
$$= 118 + 5$$
$$= 123$$

$$236 + 158 = 236 + 100 + 50 + 8$$
$$= 336 + 50 + 8$$
$$= 386 + 8$$
$$= 394$$

Use jottings to work out.

1. $62 + 35$
2. $37 + 32$
3. $59 + 23$
4. $36 + 38$
5. $47 + 45$
6. $115 + 26$
7. $124 + 59$
8. $146 + 47$
9. $118 + 54$
10. $137 + 48$
11. $127 + 124$
12. $166 + 119$

B

Use jottings to work out.

1. $69 + 65$
2. $84 + 58$
3. $78 + 46$
4. $96 + 87$
5. $59 + 54$
6. $147 + 128$
7. $122 + 119$
8. $215 + 177$
9. $359 + 126$
10. $338 + 225$
11. $273 + 462$
12. $356 + 391$

13.

348	214	
126	147	

Copy the grids.
Add the rows. ↔
Add the columns. ↕

14.

156	119	
217	237	

C

Use jottings to work out.

1. $287 + 148$
2. $368 + 175$
3. $458 + 263$
4. $386 + 275$
5. $498 + 388$
6. $579 + 147$
7. $388 + 264$
8. $567 + 296$
9. $488 + 356$
10. $547 + 377$
11. $489 + 385$
12. $576 + 296$

13.

168	188	
179	376	

Copy the grids.
Add the rows.
Add the columns.
Find the overall totals.

14.

278	289	
179	177	

On this page you will begin to develop a standard method for addition.

Examples

```
    46         174        383      Line up units with units.
  + 38       +  52      +  39      Line up tens with tens.
  ----       -----      -----
    14           6         12      Add the units.
    70         120        110      Add the tens.
    84         100        300      Add the hundreds.
  ----       -----      -----
               226        422      Find the total.
             -----      -----
```

A

Copy and complete.

1   33   **7**   55
      + 24   + 37

2   42   **8**   49
      + 25   + 45

3   37   **9**   56
      + 32   + 27

4   51   **10** 58
      + 28   + 39

5   65   **11** 47
      + 33   + 36

6   38   **12** 53
      + 26   + 28

13 Lee has 49 conkers. He finds 27 more. How many conkers does he have?

B

Copy and complete.

1   35   **8**   89
      + 28   + 35

2   46   **9**   74
      + 27   + 68

3   48   **10** 97
      + 36   + 84

4   57   **11** 168
      + 37   + 57

5   49   **12** 185
      + 39   + 67

6   66   **13** 276
      + 45   + 59

7   58   **14** 237
      + 54   + 93

C

Set out as in the examples.

1 164 + 47

2 179 + 59

3 286 + 28

4 348 + 79

5 297 + 38

6 296 + 46

7 376 + 69

8 468 + 86

9 295 + 48

10 589 + 77

11 Sanjay buys a computer for £475 and a printer for £89. How much does he spend altogether?

On this page you will learn to use two informal written methods for subtraction.

COUNTING UP

Example

$$835$$
$$-274$$

Count up	6	to make 280
	20	to make 300
	500	to make 800
	35	to make 835
Total	561	

COMPENSATION

This means take too much away and then add on.

Example

$$835$$
$$-274 \quad (274 = 300 - 26)$$
$$535 \quad \text{Take } 300$$
$$26 \quad \text{Add } 26$$
$$561$$

A

Use the counting up method.   Use the compensation method.

| **1** | 37 | **3** | 62 | **5** | 73 | **7** | 46 | **9** | 53 | **11** | 95 |
| | − 18 | | − 48 | | − 56 | | − 29 | | − 28 | | − 58 |

| **2** | 53 | **4** | 86 | **6** | 97 | **8** | 72 | **10** | 61 | **12** | 84 |
| | − 35 | | − 42 | | − 31 | | − 37 | | − 22 | | − 36 |

B

Find the difference between each pair of numbers.

Use counting up.   Use compensation.

1	67	34	**5**	143	75	**9**	85	37	**13**	247	95
2	94	48	**6**	125	49	**10**	75	48	**14**	437	56
3	181	97	**7**	158	64	**11**	154	86	**15**	322	73
4	136	83	**8**	132	77	**12**	163	75	**16**	256	68

C

Set out as in the examples.

Use counting up.   Use compensation.

1	245 − 138	**5**	769 − 383	**9**	418 − 182	**13**	883 − 249
2	363 − 187	**6**	884 − 259	**10**	634 − 277	**14**	555 − 128
3	627 − 264	**7**	935 − 472	**11**	542 − 355	**15**	727 − 464
4	541 − 425	**8**	629 − 367	**12**	875 − 491	**16**	869 − 386

On this page you will begin to learn to use decomposition.

Examples

$$73 = 70+3 = 60+13$$
$$-36 \quad\quad 30+6 \quad\quad 30+6$$
$$\overline{} \quad\quad \overline{30+7} = 37$$

$$227 = 200+20+7 = 100+120+7$$
$$-54 \quad\quad\quad 50+4 \quad\quad\quad 50+4$$
$$\overline{100+70+3} = 173$$

Check answers with addition.

$$37 \quad\quad 173$$
$$+36 \quad\quad +54$$
$$\overline{73} \quad\quad \overline{227}$$

A

Copy and complete.

1　58　　**7**　45
　　−23　　　−33

2　76　　**8**　68
　　−34　　　−25

3　84　　**9**　74
　　−21　　　−42

4　69　　**10**　57
　　−35　　　−34

5　93　　**11**　89
　　−23　　　−52

6　72　　**12**　96
　　−23　　　−51

13 Polly has 75p.
She spends 32p.
How much does she
have left?

B

Copy and complete.

1　72　　**8**　94
　　−28　　　−55

2　85　　**9**　63
　　−38　　　−38

3　64　　**10**　76
　　−49　　　−57

4　97　　**11**　55
　　−58　　　−29

5　73　　**12**　91
　　−45　　　−48

6　81　　**13**　82
　　−37　　　−65

7　62　　**14**　87
　　−24　　　−59

C

Find the difference between each pair of numbers. Set out as in the examples.

1 482 and 36
2 245 and 29
3 366 and 37
4 173 and 68
5 259 and 73
6 317 and 75
7 549 and 84
8 428 and 91
9 391 and 56
10 264 and 38
11 37 and 255
12 45 and 372
13 62 and 127
14 36 and 463
15 81 and 335
16 594 and 55

On these pages you will learn to understand the operation of multiplication.

Multiplication can be done in any order.

Example 1

3 rows of 4 squares.

$3 \times 4 = 12$

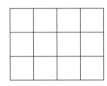

4 columns of 3 squares.

$4 \times 3 = 12$

Example 2

2 rows of 5 squares.

$2 \times 5 = 10$

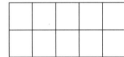

5 columns of 2 squares.

$5 \times 2 = 10$

Multiplication is the inverse of division.
Knowing one $\times$ or $\div$ fact means that you know 3 related facts.

Example 1

$6 \times 3 = 18$ $3 \times 6 = 18$
$18 \div 3 = 6$ $18 \div 6 = 3$

Example 2

$4 \times \square = 28$

The answer is 7 because $28 \div 4 = 7$.

A

Write two multiplication facts for each rectangle, as in the example.

1 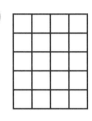   **5**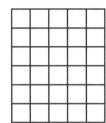

2   **6**

3   **7**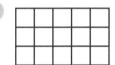

4 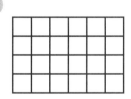   **8**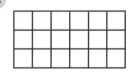

Copy and complete.

9 $7 \times \square = 14$

10 $8 \times \square = 40$

11 $\square \times 10 = 40$

12 $\square \times 2 = 18$

13 $5 \times \square = 25$

14 $9 \times \square = 90$

15 $\square \times 2 = 16$

16 $\square \times 5 = 30$

B

Use squared paper.
Draw a rectangle to show each of the multiplication facts below.
As in the example on page 40, write two facts for each rectangle.

1 2×7 **5** 5×8

2 7×5 **6** 5×6

3 8×2 **7** 8×4

4 3×7 **8** 6×7

Copy and complete each table.

9

$\times 2$
$3 \rightarrow 6$
$\rightarrow 16$
$\rightarrow 12$
$\rightarrow 18$

11

$\times 4$
$4 \rightarrow 16$
$\rightarrow 28$
$\rightarrow 40$
$\rightarrow 36$

10

$\times 3$
$5 \rightarrow 15$
$\rightarrow 27$
$\rightarrow 18$
$\rightarrow 24$

12

$\times 5$
$6 \rightarrow 30$
$\rightarrow 40$
$\rightarrow 35$
$\rightarrow 45$

Write three related facts using the same three numbers.

13 $8 \times 5 = 40$

$\square \times \square = 40$

$\square \div \square = 8$

$\square \div \square = 5$

15 $7 \times 10 = 70$

$\square \times \square = \square$

$\square \div \square = \square$

$\square \div \square = \square$

14 $6 \times 4 = 24$

$\square \times \square = 24$

$\square \div \square = 4$

$\square \div \square = 6$

16 $9 \times 3 = 27$

$\square \times \square = \square$

$\square \div \square = \square$

$\square \div \square = \square$

C

Copy and complete the multiplication squares.

1

$\times$	2		
		80	30
5			15
		56	

2

$\times$		9	
			36
7			42
	32	36	

3

$\times$		7	
			24
	45	63	
8			48

Write four different $\times$ or $\div$ facts for each group of numbers.

4 5 7 35   **8** 6 9 54

5 4 8 32   **9** 5 20 100

6 7 63 9   **10** 8 72 9

7 21 63 3   **11** 42 6 7

Copy and complete.

12 $\square \times 7 = 49$ **16** $\square \times 1 = 15$

13 $\square \times 5 = 100$ **17** $\square \times 8 = 88$

14 $4 \times \square = 0$ **18** $9 \times \square = 81$

15 $8 \times \square = 64$ **19** $5 \times \square = 125$

20 How many years are there in 60 months?

On these pages you will learn to understand division as:

- sharing.

Example

Share 18 marbles equally between 6 children?

○○○ ○○○ ○○○
○○○ ○○○ ○○○ $18 \div 6 = 3$

- grouping (or repeated subtraction).

Example

How many boxes of 6 can be filled from 18 eggs?

Hop back in 6s from 18.

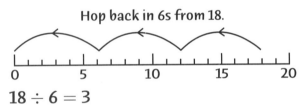

$18 \div 6 = 3$

- the inverse of multiplication.
Knowing one × or ÷ fact means that you know 3 related facts.

Example 1

$18 \div 3 = 6$ $18 \div 6 = 3$
$6 \times 3 = 18$ $3 \times 6 = 18$

Example 2

$\boxed{} \div 7 = 4$
The answer is 28 because
$4 \times 7 = 28$.

Ⓐ

Use counters. Find:

1 12 divided by 2
2 15 divided by 3
3 16 divided by 4
4 10 divided by 5
5 18 divided by 2
6 12 divided by 3.

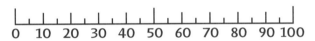

Use the number line to work out:

7 How many 10s make 40?
8 How many 5s make 35?
9 How many 20s make 60?
10 How many 10s make 70?

11 How many 5s make 55?
12 How many 20s make 100?
13 How many 15s make 60?
14 How many 25s make 75?

Copy and complete.

15 $14 \div \boxed{} = 7$
16 $40 \div \boxed{} = 8$
17 $\boxed{} \div 10 = 3$
18 $\boxed{} \div 2 = 5$

19 $30 \div \boxed{} = 6$
20 $90 \div \boxed{} = 9$
21 $\boxed{} \div 2 = 4$
22 $\boxed{} \div 5 = 7$

B

Copy and complete the tables.

1

÷2
14 →
20 →
→ 8
→ 6

3

÷4
36 →
28 →
→ 4
→ 8

2

÷5
40 →
25 →
→ 9
→ 6

4

÷3
24 →
30 →
→ 7
→ 9

Write three related facts using the same three numbers.

5 $24 \div 4 = 6$

☐ ÷ ☐ = ☐
☐ × ☐ = ☐
☐ × ☐ = ☐

7 $42 \div 6 = 7$

☐ ÷ ☐ = ☐
☐ × ☐ = ☐
☐ × ☐ = ☐

6 $24 \div 3 = 8$

☐ ÷ ☐ = ☐
☐ × ☐ = ☐
☐ × ☐ = ☐

8 $72 \div 8 = 9$

☐ ÷ ☐ = ☐
☐ × ☐ = ☐
☐ × ☐ = ☐

Copy and complete.

9 $18 \div ☐ = 2$

10 $35 \div ☐ = 5$

11 $☐ \div 8 = 1$

12 $☐ \div 10 = 10$

13 $20 \div ☐ = 5$

14 $7 \div ☐ = 7$

15 $☐ \div 6 = 5$

16 $☐ \div 4 = 20$

C

Write four different × or ÷ statements for each group of numbers.

1 8 9 72

2 6 54 9

3 8 56 7

4 63 7 9

5 2 24 48

6 4 28 7

7 21 84 4

8 48 6 8

12 can be divided in 6 different ways.

$12 \div 1 = 12$ $12 \div 4 = 3$

$12 \div 2 = 6$ $12 \div 6 = 2$

$12 \div 3 = 4$ $12 \div 12 = 1$

9 Find 6 ways of dividing:

a) 18   c) 28

b) 45   d) 50.

10 Find 8 ways of dividing:

a) 24   c) 30

b) 42   d) 54.

Copy and complete.

11 $36 \div ☐ = 6$

12 $42 \div ☐ = 6$

13 $☐ \div 9 = 4$

14 $☐ \div 7 = 7$

15 $120 \div ☐ = 20$

16 $12 \div ☐ = 12$

17 $☐ \div 8 = 8$

18 $☐ \div 3 = 31$

19 $75 \div ☐ = 25$

20 $81 \div ☐ = 9$

21 $☐ \div 4 = 1$

22 $☐ \div 10 = 50$

On this page you will learn to use the vocabulary of multiplication.

A

Write a number sentence for each problem and work out the answer.

1. What is 6 times 2?
2. Multiply 5 by 7.
3. What is 10 multiplied by 8?
4. What is 9 lots of 2?
5. Find 6 groups of 5.
6. What is 10 times as big as 4?
7. 8 children wear boots. How many boots are there?
8. Each bag holds 10 sweets. How many sweets are there in 6 bags?
9. 5 children sit at each table. There are 5 tables. How many children are there?
10. Joan is 8. Her mother is 5 times older. How old is Joan's mother?

B

Write a number sentence for each problem and work out the answer.

1. Multiply 3 by 8.
2. What is 5 times 100?
3. What is 21 multiplied by 2?
4. Find 3 lots of 40.
5. Find the product of 7 and 3.
6. What is 9 times greater than 4?
7. Rosie has 6 pens. Luke has three times as many. How many pens does Luke have?
8. A tree is 8 times taller than a fence. The fence is 2 m tall. How tall is the tree?
9. There are 6 eggs in a box. There are 5 boxes. How many eggs are there?
10. There are 12 cubes in a block. There are 3 blocks. How many cubes are there?

C

1. Look at the numbers in the box.

| 3 | 8 | 15 | 20 | 24 |

a. What is the smallest number times the largest number?
b. Multiply the middle number by the second largest.
c. What is the second smallest number multiplied by itself?
d. Which number is five times greater than the smallest number?
e. Which number is three lots of the second smallest number?
f. Ten different products can be made using pairs of the five numbers. Can you find them all?

On this page you will learn to use the vocabulary of division.

A

Write a number sentence for each problem and work out the answer.

1. Share 18 by 2.
2. Divide 70 by 10.
3. What is 45 divided by 5?
4. How many 2s make 14?
5. Share 20 by 5.
6. Divide 20 by 2.
7. What is 50 divided by 10?
8. How many 5s make 35?
9. Five children share 40 sweets equally between them. How many sweets does each child have?
10. There are 30 children in a class. Half the children have a skateboard. How many children do not have a skateboard?

B

Write a number sentence for each problem and work out the answer.

1. How many teams of 4 can be made from 32 children?

2. 90 cm of string is cut into 3 equal lengths. How long is each length?
3. 5 people win a competition. They share the £1000 prize between them. How much should each person get?
4. There are 24 children in a class.
   a) 1 in every 2 children is a boy. How many boys are there?
   b) 1 in every 3 has fair hair. How many children have fair hair?
   c) 1 in every 4 has green eyes. How many children have green eyes?

C

Write a number sentence for each problem and work out the answer.

1. A pack of 8 cans of drink costs £6.00. How much does each can of drink cost?
2. There are 48 passengers on a bus.
   a) 1 in every 6 is a girl. How many passengers are girls?
   b) 1 in every 3 is a man. How many passengers are men?
   c) 1 in every 8 is a boy. How many passengers are boys?
   d) 3 in every 8 are women. How many passengers are women?
3. A tray of plants holds 6 flowers. How many trays can be filled from 54 flowers?

On these pages you will:

- practise doubling and halving.

Examples

Double 35   = Double 30 + Double 5 = 60 + 10 = 70
Double 350 = Double 300 + Double 50 = 600 + 100 = 700
Half of 90   = Half of 100 − Half of 10 = 50 − 5 = 45
Half of 900 = Half of 800 + Half of 100 = 400 + 50 = 450

- use doubling and halving to solve calculations.

Examples

Find the 6× table by doubling the 3× table.

3s		6s
3	×1	6
6	×2	12
9	×3	18
and so on		

Work out multiples of 15 by doubling.
$1 \times 15 = 15$
$2 \times 15 = 30$
$4 \times 15 = 60$
$8 \times 15 = 120$
$16 \times 15 = 240$

Find quarters and eighths by halving.
$\frac{1}{2}$ of 280 = 140
$\frac{1}{4}$ of 280 = 70
$\frac{1}{8}$ of 280 = 35

A

Write the answers only.

1 15×2
2 7×2
3 45×2
4 30×2
5 13×2

6 8×2
7 20×2
8 14×2
9 35×2
10 50×2

11 $20 \div 2$
12 $14 \div 2$
13 $90 \div 2$
14 $6 \div 2$
15 $50 \div 2$

16 $40 \div 2$
17 $8 \div 2$
18 $100 \div 2$
19 $70 \div 2$
20 $18 \div 2$

Copy and complete.

21 $1 \times 10 = \boxed{}$
$2 \times 10 = \boxed{}$
$4 \times 10 = \boxed{}$
$8 \times 10 = \boxed{}$
$16 \times 10 = \boxed{}$

22 $1 \times 25 = \boxed{}$
$2 \times 25 = \boxed{}$
$4 \times 25 = \boxed{}$
$8 \times 25 = \boxed{}$
$16 \times 25 = \boxed{}$

Copy and complete to ×10.

23

TWOS		FOURS
2	×1	4
4	×2	8
6	×3	12
and so on to ×10		

B

Double these numbers.

1 450	**5** 20	**9** 45			
2 16	**6** 1000	**10** 75			
3 55	**7** 85	**11** 150			
4 250	**8** 500	**12** 19			

Halve these numbers.

13 700	**17** 68	**21** 170
14 130	**18** 380	**22** 26
15 260	**19** 600	**23** 800
16 800	**20** 34	**24** 190

25 Work out the 6× table by doubling the 3× table.

26 Work out the 8× table by doubling the 4× table.

27 Find one quarter of:

a) 120   e) 160

b) 600   f) 36

c) 24   g) 200

d) 1000   h) 28.

28 Copy and complete by doubling.

a) $1 \times 20 = \square$ b) $1 \times 75 = \square$
  $2 \times 20 = \square$ $2 \times 75 = \square$
  $4 \times 20 = \square$ $4 \times 75 = \square$
  $8 \times 20 = \square$ $8 \times 75 = \square$
  $16 \times 20 = \square$ $16 \times 75 = \square$

C

Double these numbers.

1 26	**5** 470	**9** 3500	**13** 34	**17** 270	**21** 4400
2 320	**6** 2400	**10** 29	**14** 450	**18** 3300	**22** 49
3 5000	**7** 58	**11** 360	**15** 2800	**19** 38	**23** 430
4 37	**8** 230	**12** 4600	**16** 44	**20** 310	**24** 3900

Find $\frac{1}{2}$ of:

25 26	**29** 920
26 580	**30** 5200
27 7600	**31** 740
28 54	**32** 94.

Find $\frac{1}{4}$ of:

33 52	**37** 960
34 5600	**38** 84
35 76	**39** 6800
36 720	**40** 92.

Find $\frac{1}{8}$ of:

41 72	**45** 400
42 1200	**46** 56
43 640	**47** 3600
44 96	**48** 480.

49 Work out the 12 times table by doubling the 6 times table.

50 Work out the 16 times table by doubling the 8 times table.

51 Work out multiples of 13 to 16 × 13. Use to work out.

a 9×13 b 24×13 c 7×13 d 18×13 e 27×13

On this page you will revise the multiplication and division facts for 2, 5 and 10.

A

Write the answers only.

1. 6×2
2. 9×2
3. 1×2
4. 8×2

5. 8×5
6. 0×5
7. 7×5
8. 6×5

9. 10×10
10. 7×10
11. 9×10
12. 8×10

13. $8 \div 2$
14. $14 \div 2$
15. $20 \div 2$
16. $18 \div 2$

17. $50 \div 5$
18. $25 \div 5$
19. $45 \div 5$
20. $30 \div 5$

21. $30 \div 10$
22. $10 \div 10$
23. $90 \div 10$
24. $60 \div 10$

B

Copy and complete.

1. $\square \times 2 = 8$
2. $\square \times 5 = 25$
3. $8 \times \square = 80$
4. $8 \times \square = 16$

5. $\square \times 5 = 0$
6. $\square \times 10 = 60$
7. $6 \times \square = 12$
8. $10 \times \square = 50$

9. $\square \times 10 = 90$
10. $\square \times 2 = 2$
11. $8 \times \square = 40$
12. $3 \times \square = 3$

13. $\square \div 5 = 6$
14. $\square \div 10 = 7$
15. $10 \div \square = 5$
16. $10 \div \square = 2$

17. $\square \div 10 = 4$
18. $\square \div 2 = 9$
19. $45 \div \square = 9$
20. $100 \div \square = 10$

21. $\square \div 2 = 7$
22. $\square \div 5 = 7$
23. $10 \div \square = 1$
24. $20 \div \square = 10$

C

Work out the brackets first. Write the answers only.

1. $(3 \times 2) + (5 \times 5)$
2. $(6 \times 10) + (7 \times 2)$
3. $(8 \times 5) + (8 \times 10)$
4. $(9 \times 10) + (2 \times 5)$

5. $(5 \times 2) + (3 \times 10)$
6. $(10 \times 5) + (9 \times 2)$
7. $(9 \times 5) - (4 \times 2)$
8. $(5 \times 10) - (4 \times 5)$

9. $(7 \times 10) - (10 \times 2)$
10. $(4 \times 10) - (7 \times 5)$
11. $(6 \times 5) - (6 \times 2)$
12. $(10 \times 10) - (8 \times 2)$

Copy and complete the multiplication squares.

13.

×	2	5	10
7	14		70
8			
5			

14.

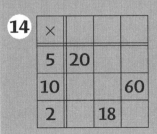

×			
5	20		
10			60
2		18	

On this page you will practise the multiplication and division facts for 3.

A

Write out the 3 times table.

Work out:

1. 4×3
2. 7×3
3. 0×3
4. 5×3
5. 8×3

6. 3×3
7. 10×3
8. 6×3
9. 9×3
10. 1×3

11. $6 \div 3$
12. $12 \div 3$
13. $21 \div 3$
14. $9 \div 3$
15. $30 \div 3$

16. $18 \div 3$
17. $27 \div 3$
18. $3 \div 3$
19. $15 \div 3$
20. $24 \div 3$

21. 3×10
22. 3×6
23. 3×9
24. 3×5
25. 3×8.

B

Write the answers only.

1. 5×3
2. 6×3
3. 3×3
4. 0×3
5. 8×3

6. 4×3
7. 9×3
8. 1×3
9. 7×3

10. $12 \div 3$
11. $30 \div 3$
12. $6 \div 3$
13. $18 \div 3$
14. $27 \div 3$

15. $9 \div 3$
16. $24 \div 3$
17. $15 \div 3$
18. $21 \div 3$

Copy and complete.

19. $\square \times 3 = 6$
20. $\square \times 3 = 21$
21. $\square \times 3 = 3$
22. $\square \times 3 = 18$

23. $\square \times 3 = 30$
24. $\square \times 3 = 24$
25. $\square \times 3 = 0$
26. $\square \times 3 = 27$

27. $\square \div 3 = 3$
28. $\square \div 3 = 6$
29. $\square \div 3 = 4$
30. $\square \div 3 = 7$

31. $\square \div 3 = 9$
32. $\square \div 3 = 5$
33. $\square \div 3 = 1$
34. $\square \div 3 = 8$

C

Write the answers only.

1. 30×3
2. 50×3
3. 90×3
4. 60×3
5. 200×3

6. 40×3
7. 70×3
8. 20×3
9. 80×3
10. 25×3

11. $150 \div 3$
12. $60 \div 3$
13. $240 \div 3$
14. $300 \div 3$
15. $210 \div 3$

16. $90 \div 3$
17. $270 \div 3$
18. $30 \div 3$
19. $120 \div 3$
20. $180 \div 3$

Work out by multiplying by 3 and doubling.

21. 4×6
22. 8×6
23. 7×6
24. 6×6
25. 9×6

26. 20×6
27. 50×6
28. 40×6
29. 30×6
30. 60×6

31. Three silver stars wins a gold star. Aaron has 15 gold stars. How many silver stars has he won?

32. There are 12 eggs in each box. How many eggs are there in three boxes?

On this page you will practise the multiplication and division facts for 4.

A

Write out the 4 times table.

Work out:

1 1×4
2 9×4
3 6×4
4 10×4
5 3×4

6 8×4
7 5×4
8 0×4
9 7×4
10 4×4

11 $12 \div 4$
12 $40 \div 4$
13 $24 \div 4$
14 $36 \div 4$
15 $4 \div 4$

16 $32 \div 4$
17 $8 \div 4$
18 $20 \div 4$
19 $28 \div 4$
20 $16 \div 4$

21 4×5
22 4×8
23 4×6
24 4×9
25 4×7

B

Write the answers only.

1 3×4
2 4×4
3 9×4
4 6×4
5 1×4

6 8×4
7 5×4
8 0×4
9 7×4

10 $8 \div 4$
11 $28 \div 4$
12 $12 \div 4$
13 $40 \div 4$
14 $20 \div 4$

15 $36 \div 4$
16 $16 \div 4$
17 $24 \div 4$
18 $32 \div 4$

Copy and complete.

19 $\square \times 4 = 28$
20 $\square \times 4 = 8$
21 $\square \times 4 = 24$
22 $\square \times 4 = 4$

23 $\square \times 4 = 36$
24 $\square \times 4 = 0$
25 $\square \times 4 = 40$
26 $\square \times 4 = 32$

27 $\square \div 4 = 6$
28 $\square \div 4 = 4$
29 $\square \div 4 = 3$
30 $\square \div 4 = 7$

31 $\square \div 4 = 5$
32 $\square \div 4 = 9$
33 $\square \div 4 = 1$
34 $\square \div 4 = 8$

C

Write the answers only.

1 20×4
2 70×4
3 40×4
4 30×4
5 90×4

6 50×4
7 80×4
8 60×4
9 200×4
10 500×4

11 $120 \div 4$
12 $240 \div 4$
13 $40 \div 4$
14 $320 \div 4$
15 $160 \div 4$

16 $400 \div 4$
17 $80 \div 4$
18 $200 \div 4$
19 $280 \div 4$
20 $360 \div 4$

Work out by multiplying by 4 and doubling.

21 3×8
22 7×8
23 9×8
24 6×8
25 8×8

26 40×8
27 20×8
28 50×8
29 30×8
30 60×8

31 A school has 100 children equally divided into four classes. How many children are there in each class?

32 There are 150 tissues in a box. How many tissues are there in 4 boxes?

On this page you will learn to understand the idea of a remainder.

Example

13 marbles are shared
equally between 3 children.

OO OO OO
OO OO OO O

Each child gets 4 marbles and
there is one marble left over.

$13 \div 3 = 4$ r. 1 (4 remainder 1)

A

Copy and complete.

1 $9 = 4 \times 2 + \square$

2 $27 = 5 \times 5 + \square$

3 $34 = 3 \times 10 + \square$

4 $62 = 6 \times 10 + \square$

5 $13 = 6 \times 2 + \square$

6 $37 = 7 \times 5 + \square$

7 $51 = 10 \times 5 + \square$

8 $97 = 9 \times 10 + \square$

9 $17 = 8 \times 2 + \square$

10 $11 = 5 \times 2 + \square$

11 $42 = 8 \times 5 + \square$

12 $83 = 8 \times 10 + \square$

13 $58 = 5 \times 10 + \square$

14 $19 = 9 \times 2 + \square$

15 $49 = 9 \times 5 + \square$

16 $31 = 6 \times 5 + \square$

17 $79 = 7 \times 10 + \square$

18 $15 = 7 \times 2 + \square$

19 $17 = 5 \times 3 + \square$

20 $42 = 10 \times 4 + \square$

B

Copy and complete.

1 $16 \div 3 = 5$ r. $\square$

2 $19 \div 7 = 2$ r. $\square$

3 $37 \div 4 = 9$ r. $\square$

4 $22 \div 6 = 3$ r. $\square$

5 $20 \div 3 = 6$ r. $\square$

6 $35 \div 8 = 4$ r. $\square$

7 $27 \div 4 = 6$ r. $\square$

8 $49 \div 9 = 5$ r. $\square$

9 $25 \div 3 = 8$ r. $\square$

10 $38 \div 7 = \square$ r. $\square$

11 $29 \div 4 = \square$ r. $\square$

12 $26 \div 6 = \square$ r. $\square$

13 $29 \div 3 = \square$ r. $\square$

14 $43 \div 4 = \square$ r. $\square$

15 $21 \div 8 = \square$ r. $\square$

16 $34 \div 4 = \square$ r. $\square$

17 $22 \div 3 = \square$ r. $\square$

18 $34 \div 9 = \square$ r. $\square$

19 $57 \div 5 = \square$ r. $\square$

20 $25 \div 7 = \square$ r. $\square$

C

Copy and complete.

1 $\square \div 6 = 6$ r. 2

2 $\square \div 7 = 6$ r. 2

3 $\square \div 8 = 8$ r. 2

4 $\square \div 9 = 9$ r. 2

5 $\square \div 6 = 8$ r. 3

6 $\square \div 7 = 9$ r. 6

7 $\square \div 8 = 9$ r. 1

8 $\square \div 9 = 8$ r. 8

9 $\square \div 6 = 3$ r. 1

10 $\square \div 7 = 5$ r. 3

11 $\square \div 8 = 7$ r. 5

12 $\square \div 9 = 10$ r. 3

13 $\square \div 6 = 9$ r. 5

14 $\square \div 7 = 8$ r. 4

15 $\square \div 8 = 6$ r. 4

16 $\square \div 9 = 4$ r. 7

17 $\square \div 6 = 7$ r. 4

18 $\square \div 9 = 6$ r. 5

19 $\square \div 5 = 18$ r. 2

20 $\square \div 4 = 23$ r. 3

On these pages you will learn to make sensible decisions about rounding up or down after division.

Examples

Tickets cost £5.

I have £34.

How many tickets can I buy?

$34 \div 5 = 6$ remainder 4.

Answer: I can buy 6 tickets.

A car can carry 5 people.

34 people need transport.

How many cars are needed?

$34 \div 5 = 6$ remainder 4.

Answer: 7 cars are needed.

A relay team needs 4 runners.

There are 22 runners.

How many teams can be made?

$22 \div 4 = 5$ remainder 2

Answer: 5 teams can be made.

4 children sit at each table.

There are 22 children.

How many tables are needed?

$22 \div 4 = 5$ remainder 2

Answer: 6 tables are needed.

A

Write the answers only.

1 Two children can sit at each table. There are 17 children. How many tables are needed?

2 There are 28 children at a football club. How many 5-a-side teams can be made?

3 Ten children can sit on a bench. There are 68 children. How many benches are needed?

4 One lollipop costs 10p. I have 24p. How many lollipops can I buy?

5 Dean saves £2 every week. How long will it take him to save £11.

6 There are 15 children at a tennis club. How many pairs of children can be made?

7 A baker makes 47 cakes. Five cakes can fit into one box. How many boxes are needed?

8 A florist has 93 flowers. A bunch of flowers has ten flowers. How many bunches can she make?

B

1. Zoe has 108 pens.
   Each packet holds 10 pens.
   How many packets does she need?

2. Derek can saw 3 boards from each plank. How many planks are needed to saw 25 boards?

3. A tennis coach has 42 tennis balls. Each box holds four balls. How many boxes does he need?

4. There are 30 children in a P.E. lesson. How many teams of four can be made?

5. There are 27 children in a class. Six children can sit at each table. How many tables are needed?

6. Cans of drink are sold in packs of four. There are 26 cans. How many packs of four can be made?

7. The 28 children in a class need rubbers. Each box holds 8 rubbers. How many boxes does the teacher need to collect?

8. Marcus has £20.
   Books cost £3 each.
   How many books can Marcus buy?

C

1. 230 children are going on a trip. Each coach can carry 50 children.
   How many coaches are needed?

2. Rolls are sold in packets of 8. A baker has 46 rolls.
   How many packets can he make?

3. The 190 pupils in a school need a Maths exercise book. The books are sold in packs of 20. How many packs are needed?

4. A farmer has 46 eggs.
   A box holds 6 eggs.
   How many boxes can be filled?

5. 210 tickets have been sold for a school concert.
   25 chairs make one row.
   How many rows of chairs are needed?

6. 40 children want to play netball. Each team has 7 players.
   How many teams can be made?

7. There are 148 empty bottles.
   Each crate holds 20 bottles.
   How many crates are needed?

8. Kerry has £50.
   C.D.s cost £9 each.
   How many C.D.s can she buy?

On this page you will learn to multiply or divide by 1, 10 or 100.

Examples

$4 \times 1 = 4$ $4 \times 10 = 40$ $4 \times 100 = 400$

$400 \div 1 = 400$ $400 \div 10 = 40$ $400 \div 100 = 4$

A

Copy and complete by filling in the boxes.

1 $2 \times 1 = \Box$
$2 \times 10 = \Box$
$2 \times 100 = \Box$

2 $3 \times 1 = \Box$
$3 \times 10 = \Box$
$3 \times 100 = \Box$

3 $4 \times 1 = \Box$
$4 \times 10 = \Box$
$4 \times 100 = \Box$

4 $\Box \div 1 = 3$
$\Box \div 10 = 3$
$\Box \div 100 = 3$

5 $\Box \div 1 = 5$
$\Box \div 10 = 5$
$\Box \div 100 = 5$

6 $\Box \div 100 = 6$
$\Box \div 10 = 6$
$\Box \div 1 = 6$

B

Write the answers only.

1 5×1
2 2×10
3 1×100
4 $800 \div 10$
5 $600 \div 100$
6 6×10
7 $4 \div 1$
8 5×100
9 $60 \div 10$
10 9×1

Copy and complete.

11 $9 \times \Box = 900$
12 $4 \times \Box = 4$
13 $7 \times \Box = 70$
14 $\Box \times 1 = 3$
15 $\Box \times 100 = 800$
16 $\Box \times 10 = 40$
17 $1000 \div \Box = 10$
18 $80 \div \Box = 8$
19 $9 \div \Box = 9$
20 $\Box \div 10 = 50$
21 $\Box \div 1 = 6$
22 $\Box \div 100 = 7$

C

Write the answers only.

1 14×10
2 19×1
3 25×100
4 $13 \div 1$
5 $240 \div 10$
6 $4200 \div 100$
7 36×1
8 52×100
9 $1800 \div 100$
10 $270 \div 10$

Copy and complete.

11 $24 \times \Box = 2400$
12 $56 \times \Box = 56$
13 $63 \times \Box = 630$
14 $93 \div \Box = 93$
15 $5200 \div \Box = 52$
16 $670 \div \Box = 67$
17 $\Box \times 1 = 82$
18 $\Box \times 100 = 1400$
19 $\Box \times 10 = 390$
20 $\Box \div 100 = 38$
21 $\Box \div 1 = 45$
22 $\Box \div 10 = 780$

On this page you will learn to multiply a multiple of 10 by a single digit number.

Examples

$20 \times 3 = 60$ $30 \times 4 = 120$ $70 \times 5 = 350$

A

Copy and complete these multiplication tables.

1 $1 \times 20 = 20$
$2 \times 20 = \square$
$3 \times 20 = \square$
$4 \times 20 = \square$
$5 \times 20 = 100$

2 $1 \times 30 = \square$
$2 \times 30 = \square$
$3 \times 30 = \square$
$4 \times 30 = 120$
$5 \times 30 = \square$

3 $1 \times 40 = \square$
$2 \times 40 = \square$
$3 \times 40 = \square$
$4 \times 40 = \square$
$5 \times 40 = 200$

4 $1 \times 50 = \square$
$2 \times 50 = \square$
$3 \times 50 = 150$
$4 \times 50 = \square$
$5 \times 50 = \square$

B

Copy and complete the multiplication squares.

1

×	20	30	50
2			
3			
10			

2

×	10	20	40
4			
5			
3			

3

×	30	40	50
10			
4			
5			

Copy and complete.

4 $50 \times \square = 150$
5 $\square \times 4 = 120$
6 $40 \times \square = 200$
7 $\square \times 2 = 60$
8 $20 \times \square = 80$
9 $\square \times 3 = 120$
10 $30 \times \square = 150$
11 $\square \times 2 = 160$
12 $50 \times \square = 200$

C

Copy and complete the tables.

1

×6
$50 \rightarrow 300$
$20 \rightarrow$
$60 \rightarrow$
$\rightarrow 240$
$\rightarrow 180$
$\rightarrow 480$

2

×7
$40 \rightarrow 280$
$30 \rightarrow$
$70 \rightarrow$
$\rightarrow 350$
$\rightarrow 140$
$\rightarrow 420$

3

×8
$20 \rightarrow 160$
$40 \rightarrow$
$50 \rightarrow$
$\rightarrow 480$
$\rightarrow 240$
$\rightarrow 720$

4

×9
$60 \rightarrow 540$
$30 \rightarrow$
$80 \rightarrow$
$\rightarrow 360$
$\rightarrow 810$
$\rightarrow 450$

On this page you will learn to multiply a two-digit number by a single digit number.

Example

$23 \times 2 = (20 \times 2) + (3 \times 2)$
$\qquad = 40 + 6$
$\qquad = 46$

$16 \times 4 = (10 \times 4) + (6 \times 4)$
$\qquad = 40 + 24$
$\qquad = 64$

 A

Copy and complete.

1 $12 \times 2 = (10 \times 2) + (2 \times 2) = \square + \square = \square$

2 $31 \times 2 = (30 \times 2) + (1 \times 2) = \square + \square = \square$

3 $11 \times 3 = (10 \times 3) + (1 \times 3) = \square + \square = \square$

4 $24 \times 2 = (20 \times 2) + (4 \times 2) = \square + \square = \square$

5 $12 \times 4 = (10 \times 4) + (2 \times 4) = \square + \square = \square$

6 $43 \times 2 = (40 \times 2) + (3 \times 2) = \square + \square = \square$

7 $34 \times 3 = (30 \times 3) + (4 \times 3) = \square + \square = \square$

8 $22 \times 2 = (20 \times 2) + (2 \times 2) = \square + \square = \square$

$(20 \times 3) + (4 \times 5)$

B

Work out the following. (You can write some working.)

1 13×2
2 12×3
3 34×2
4 23×3

5 41×2
6 22×4
7 11×2
8 13×3

9 23×2
10 33×3
11 44×2
12 21×3

13 32×2
14 11×4
15 14×2
16 22×3

C

Copy and complete.

1 $46 \times 2 = \square$
2 $32 \times 4 = \square$
3 $25 \times 3 = \square$
4 $37 \times 2 = \square$
5 $34 \times 5 = \square$

6 $29 \times \square = 58$
7 $26 \times \square = 130$
8 $27 \times \square = 81$
9 $19 \times \square = 76$
10 $34 \times \square = 102$

11 $\square \times 5 = 70$
12 $\square \times 2 = 98$
13 $\square \times 3 = 54$
14 $\square \times 4 = 96$
15 $\square \times 5 = 155$

If you roll two dice you could score 7 in three different ways, but there is only one way that you could score 12.

  1 and 6 scores 7. Only 6 and 6 score 12.
  2 and 5 scores 7.
  3 and 4 scores 7.

Copy and complete this table showing the number of ways each possible number can be scored.

Score	2	3	4	5	6	7	8	9	10	11	12
Possible ways						3					1

B

If you roll three dice the highest possible score is 18. This can only be scored in one way. 14, however, can be scored in four possible ways.

  6, 6 and 2 scores 14. 6, 4 and 4 scores 14. 6, 6 and 6 scores 18.
  6, 5 and 3 scores 14. 5, 5 and 4 scores 14.

Copy and complete the table for three dice.

Score	3	4	5	6	7	8	9	10	11	12	13	14	15	16	17	18
Possible ways												4				1

C

1 If you roll two dice and multiply the numbers the highest possible score is 36 (6 × 6). Which numbers below 36 is it impossible to score?

If you roll three dice and multiply, you can score 20 in two different ways, but there is only one way you could score 100.

  $2 \times 2 \times 5 = 20$ $4 \times 5 \times 5 = 100$
  $4 \times 5 \times 1 = 20$

2 Find one way of scoring:
 a) 80 b) 216 c) 32 d) 75.

3 Find two ways of scoring:
 a) 36 b) 60 c) 48 d) 18.

On this page you will learn to recognise the operation in a number sentence.

Example   34 ☐ 2 = 68   **The missing sign is ×.**

A
Copy and complete by putting + or − in the box.
1 43 ☐ 8 = 35
2 14 ☐ 16 = 30
3 27 ☐ 18 = 9
4 37 ☐ 5 = 42
5 19 ☐ 2 = 21
6 80 ☐ 17 = 63
7 36 ☐ 7 = 29
8 55 ☐ 35 = 90

B
Copy and complete by putting +, − or × in the box.
1 65 ☐ 27 = 38
2 46 ☐ 39 = 85
3 12 ☐ 4 = 48
4 78 ☐ 25 = 103
5 160 ☐ 39 = 121
6 23 ☐ 10 = 230
7 55 ☐ 47 = 102
8 7 ☐ 3 = 21

C
Copy and complete by putting +, −, × or ÷ in the box.
1 12 ☐ 6 = 72
2 40 ☐ 5 = 8
3 36 ☐ 19 = 55
4 103 ☐ 6 = 97
5 125 ☐ 71 = 196
6 8 ☐ 7 = 56
7 120 ☐ 84 = 36
8 99 ☐ 9 = 11

Now you will learn to make up stories to match number sentences.

Example   60 − 28 = 32
Sarah had 60p. She spent 28p. She had 32p left.

Make up a story to match each of these number sentences.

A
1 15 + 12 = 27
2 24 − 13 = 11
3 8 × 10 = 80
4 16 ÷ 2 = 8
5 30 + 16 = 46
6 50 − 15 = 35
7 6 × 2 = 12
8 30 ÷ 5 = 6

B
1 54 + 46 = 100
2 40 − 17 = 23
3 24 × 5 = 120
4 36 ÷ 4 = 9
5 80 − 35 = 45
6 15 × 3 = 45
7 146 + 50 = 196
8 50 ÷ 2 = 25

C
1 84 − 36 = 48
2 30 × 4 = 120
3 64 + 48 = 112
4 66 ÷ 2 = 33
5 15 × 3 = 45
6 97 + 68 = 165
7 48 ÷ 4 = 12
8 100 − 35 = 65

On this page you will learn to give examples to match a general statement.

Example

If you add 20 to a number the units number stays the same.

$7 + 20 = 27$ $37 + 20 = 57$ $127 + 20 = 147$

 A

Give two examples to match each of these statements.

1 The order in which you add two numbers does not change the answer.

2 If you double an odd number the answer is an even number.

3 If a number ends in 0 it divides exactly by 10.

4 You can add 9 by adding 10 and taking away 1.

5 A triangle always has three sides.

B

Give three examples to match each of these statements.

1 If a number ends in 5 it divides exactly by 5.

2 The order in which you multiply two numbers does not change the answer.

3 An even number is the sum of two odd numbers.

4 A multiple of 6 is always a multiple of 3.

5 A square always has four right angles.

C

Give three examples to match each of these statements.

1 You can add 99 by adding 100 and subtracting 1.

2 The 6 times table is always even.

3 Halving and halving again is the same as dividing by 4.

4 Multiplying by 8 is the same as multiplying by 4 and doubling.

5 The opposite sides of a rectangle are always equal.

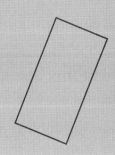

On these pages you will learn:

- to choose the operation or operations needed to solve word problems.

- to decide whether the calculation will be done mentally or on paper.

- to use all four operations to solve the problems.

Some of the problems need one operation only. Some problems need more than one operation.

Carly has 24 toys. Ryan has 13.
How many do they have altogether?

$24 + 13 = 37$

They have 37 toys altogether.

Carly has 43 felt tip pens.
Ryan has 19 more.
How many do they have altogether?

$43 + 19 = 62$
$43 + 62 = 105$

They have 105 pens altogether.

In each section read the problems and decide:

a) what operations are needed.
b) whether the calculation will be done mentally or on paper.

Then solve the problems.

A

Write the answers only.

1 There are 30 children in a class. 16 are boys. How many are girls?

2 Donna is 16 years old. Scott is half her age. How old is Scott?

3 There are 12 people on a bus. 6 get off. 10 more people get on. How many people are there now on the bus?

4 Martin has two piles of 6 books and three piles of 5 books. How many books does he have altogether?

5 Lee has 24 stickers.
Dawn has 9 more.
How many stickers does Dawn have?

6 There are 40 toys in a shop.
15 are sold on Monday.
Nine more are sold on Tuesday.
How many toys are left?

7 Five people can sit at one table. How many people can sit at seven tables?

8 20 children are asked to choose their favourite colour. 8 children choose blue. Half of the rest choose red. How many children choose a different colour?

B

1. A newsagent has 100 newspapers. He sells 68. How many newspapers are left?

2. Neil saves £4 every week. How long will it take him to save £28?

3. There are 70 apples on a tree. 25 apples are picked. 8 more fall off the tree. How many apples are left on the tree?

4. It takes Stacey four minutes to read one page. There are 20 pages in her book. How long will it take her to read the book?

5. Jamie buys three packets of 8 Christmas cards and one box of 25 cards. How many cards has he bought?

6. Helen is 33 years old. Sally is 21 years older.

   How old is Sally?

7. Darren has 23 marbles. Nathan has 12 more. How many marbles do they have altogether?

8. There are 48 biscuits in a tin. Half of them are eaten. 13 more are eaten. How many biscuits are left?

C

1. How many days are there in six weeks?

2. There are 94 passengers on a train. 59 get off. How many passengers are left on the train?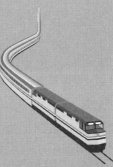

3. Sarah's book has 68 pages. She needs to read 5 more pages to reach half way. What page is she on?

4. Eight children shared 40 sweets equally between them. How many sweets did each child receive?

5. Jason has 17 more books on his top shelf than on his bottom shelf. He has 45 books on his top shelf. How many books does Jason have altogether?

6. There are 65 adults and 47 children on a train. How many people are there on the train?

7. Four classes in a school have 25 children each. The other four classes have 30 children each. How many children are there in the school?

8. There are 84 cars parked in a car park. 67 more cars are parked. 54 cars drive out. How many cars are left in the car park?

On these pages you will learn to solve money problems and to change pounds to pence and pence to pounds.

Examples

170p = £1·70   205p = £2·05

SCHOOL SHOP PRICES			
pencil	15p	T-shirt	£3·20
pen	45p	sweatshirt	£8·80
ruler	25p	dictionary	£3·75
rubber	20p	calculator	£2·50
felt tips (pack)	80p	geometry set	£4·25
crayons (pack)	75p	homework bag	£3·50
sharpener	30p	P.E. bag	£2·30

A

Change to pence.

1 £1·50   **3** £1·35

2 £1·20   **4** £1·75

Change to pounds and pence.

5 125p   **7** 130p

6 140p   **8** 165p

Work out the cost of these items and the change from £1.00.

9 4 rubbers

10 3 pencils

11 1 pen, 1 sharpener

12 2 pencils, 1 sharpener

13 2 rulers, 1 rubber

14 1 pack of felt tips, 1 pencil

15 1 pack of crayons, 1 pencil

16 2 rubbers, 1 pen

17 1 rubber, 1 sharpener

18 1 ruler, 1 sharpener

Copy and complete by writing a number in each box.

   (£1)   (50p)   (20p)   (10p)

19 ☐ × 50p   **23** ☐ × 10p   **27** ☐ × 1p   **31** ☐ × 10p

20 ☐ × 10p   **24** ☐ × 1p   **28** ☐ × 10p   **32** ☐ × 2p

21 ☐ × 1p   **25** ☐ × 5p   **29** ☐ × 2p   **33** ☐ × 5p

22 ☐ × 5p   **26** ☐ × 2p   **30** ☐ × 5p   **34** ☐ × 1p

B

Change to pence.

1 £2·30   3 £6·42

2 £3·85   4 £8·15

Change to pounds and pence.

5 235p   7 523p

6 460p   8 745p

Work out the cost of these items and the change from £5·00.

9 1 T-shirt, 4 rulers

10 1 calculator, 1 P.E. bag

11 1 geometry set, 1 pen

12 1 dictionary, 2 rubbers

13 4 packs of crayons

14 2 pens, 4 pencils

15 1 calculator, 2 pens

16 3 packs of felt tips

How many of these items can you buy for £5·00?

17 rulers   18 P.E. bags   19 rubbers   20 crayons

Copy and complete by writing the missing number in the box.

21 £10 = ☐ × 50p   25 £5 = ☐ × 50p   29 £20 = ☐ × 50p

22 £10 = ☐ × 20p   26 £5 = ☐ × 20p   30 £20 = ☐ × 20p

23 £10 = ☐ × 10p   27 £5 = ☐ × 5p   31 £20 = ☐ × 10p

24 £10 = ☐ × 5p   28 £5 = ☐ × 1p   32 £20 = ☐ × 5p

C

Change to pence.

1 £7·26   3 £3·72

2 £4·04   4 £9·08

Change to pounds and pence.

5 257p   7 516

6 349p   8 74p

Work out the cost of these items and the change from £10·00.

9 3 T-shirts

10 1 calculator, 2 pens

11 6 rubbers, 1 homework bag

12 1 sweatshirt, 3 rulers

13 30 pencils

14 1 P.E. bag, 4 sharpeners

15 8 packs of crayons

16 2 geometry sets, 1 pen

How many of these items could you buy for £10·00?

17 felt tips   18 calculators   19 pens   20 homework bags.

21 You buy a geometry set, two packs of felt tips and one other item. You pay with a £10 note and receive £3·95 change. What is the other item?

22 You buy a dictionary, a sweatshirt and one other item. You pay with a £20·00 note and receive £5·15 change. What is the other item?

On these pages you will learn to use a ruler to measure length.

Start measuring from O,
not from the end of the
ruler, and read the scale.

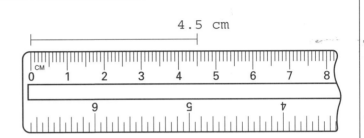

Examples

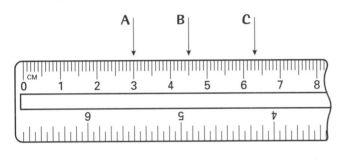

$A = 3\,cm$

$B = 4\frac{1}{2}\,cm$
$\quad= 4 \cdot 5\,cm$

$C = 6\,cm\,3\,mm$
$\quad= 6 \cdot 3\,cm$

A

Read the measurements shown on each ruler:

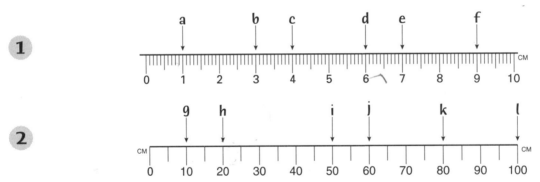

1

2

Measure these lines to the nearest centimetre.

3 |————————————————————————|

4 |————————————————|

5 |——————————————————————————|

6 |——————————————————|

7 |————————————————————|

8 |——————————————|

B

Read the measurements shown on each ruler:

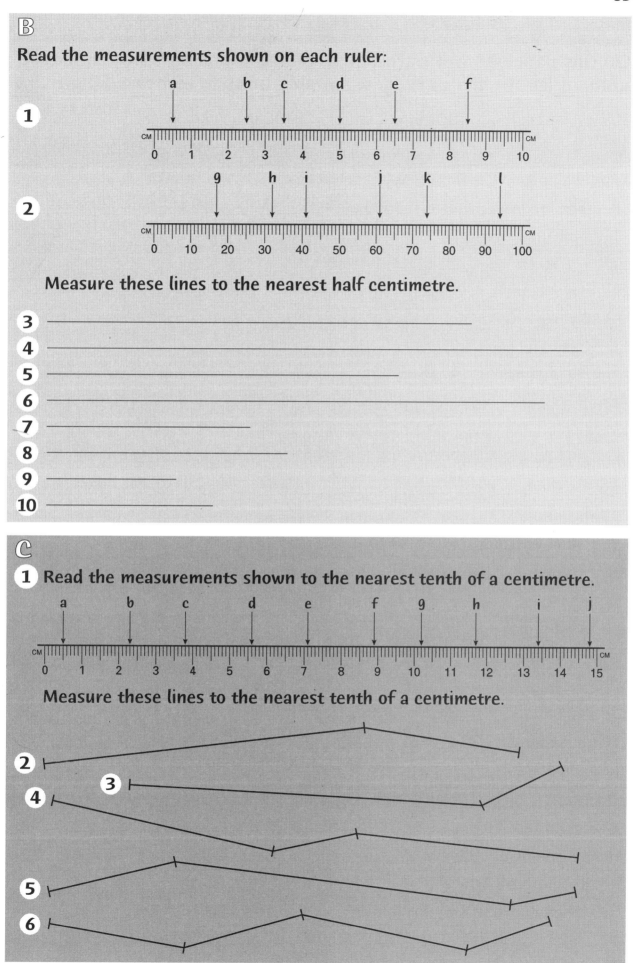

Measure these lines to the nearest half centimetre.

3 _____

4 _____

5 _____

6 _____

7 _____

8 _____

9 _____

10 _____

C

1 Read the measurements shown to the nearest tenth of a centimetre.

Measure these lines to the nearest tenth of a centimetre.

On this page you will learn to use the relationship between metric units of length and to suggest suitable units to measure lengths.

10 mm = 1 cm   100 cm = 1 m   1000 m = 1 km

A

Make 1 metre.

1 60 cm + ☐

2 20 cm + ☐

3 ☐ + 90 cm

4 ☐ + 30 cm

5 80 cm + ☐

6 50 cm + ☐

7 ☐ + 40 cm

8 ☐ + 10 cm

Would you expect these things to be longer or shorter than:

| 1 centimetre |

9 a shirt button

10 a rubber

11 an ant

12 a caterpillar

| 10 centimetres |

13 a felt tip pen

14 a finger

15 a toothbrush

16 a shoelace

| 1 metre |

17 a chair leg

18 the height of a door

19 the width of a door

20 a skipping rope.

B

Make 1 metre.

1 35 cm + ☐

2 75 cm + ☐

3 ☐ + 15 cm

4 ☐ + 55 cm

Make 1 kilometre.

5 200 m + ☐

6 600 m + ☐

7 ☐ + 300 m

8 ☐ + 900 m

Suggest a suitable metric unit to measure the length of:

9 a shoe

10 a classroom

11 the distance to the Moon

12 a car journey

13 a banana

14 a house

15 Africa

16 a running track.

C

Copy and complete.

1 72 cm + ☐ = 1 m

2 17 cm + ☐ = 1 m

3 ☐ + 58 cm = 1 m

4 ☐ + 31 cm = 1 m

5 260 m + ☐ = 1 km

6 430 m + ☐ = 1 km

7 ☐ + 50 m = 1 km

8 ☐ + 820 m = 1 km

9 4 mm + ☐ = 1 cm

10 8 mm + ☐ = 1 cm

11 ☐ + 3 mm = 1 cm

12 ☐ + 1 mm = 1 cm

Copy and complete by choosing the most sensible estimate.

13 A football pitch is about (10 m, 100 m, 100 m) long.

14 A paperback book is (2 cm, 12 cm, 20 cm) tall.

15 A front door is (1 m, 2 m, 5 m) tall.

16 A one pound coin is about (3 mm, 13 mm, 30 mm) thick.

On this page you will learn to solve problems involving length.

A

1. Sammy the snake is 63 cm long. Susan is 8 cm longer. How long is Susan?

2. Claire has two ribbons. One ribbon is 40 cm long. The second ribbon is twice as long. How long is the second ribbon?

3. A plank of wood is 90 cm long. 60 cm is sawn off. How long is the plank now?

4. A fence is 24 m long. Half of the fence has been painted. How long is the unpainted fence?

5. A block of flats is 40 m tall. A tree is 15 m shorter. How tall is the tree?

B

1. It is 200 m from Leah's house to the school. The post office is 80 m closer. How far is it from Leah's house to the post office?

2. Stuart's top shelf is 65 cm long. His bottom shelf is 23 cm longer. How long is the bottom shelf?

3. 60 cm of string is cut into 3 equal lengths. How long is each length?

4. A cyclist travels 25 km in one hour. How far does she travel in 3 hours?

5. A roller coaster is 200 metres long. Henry goes round four times. How far does he travel?

C

1. A man walks one and a half kilometres. He walks a further 400 m. How far has he walked altogether in metres.

2. A pipe is 2 m long. 80 cm is cut off. How long is the pipe which is left?

3. An athlete trains by running 800 metres five times. How far does she run in kilometres?

4. There are 20 identical books in a pile. The pile is 60 cm high. How thick is each book?

5. Harry's mother is one and a half metres tall. Harry is 27 cm shorter. How tall is Harry?

On these pages you will learn to use metric units of mass.

MASS = HEAVINESS

An elephant has a greater mass than a feather.

An elephant weighs more than a feather.

The metric units of mass are kilograms and grams.

$$1000 \, g = 1 \, kg$$
$$500 \, g = 0 \cdot 5 \, kg$$
$$= \text{half a kilogram}$$
$$100 \, g = 0 \cdot 1 \, kg$$
$$2500 \, g = 2 \cdot 5 \, kg$$
$$= 2\tfrac{1}{2} \, \text{kilograms}$$

Examples

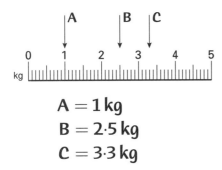

$$A = 1 \, kg$$
$$B = 2 \cdot 5 \, kg$$
$$C = 3 \cdot 3 \, kg$$

A

Write as grams.

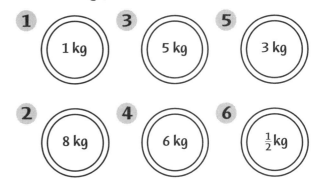

1 1 kg **3** 5 kg **5** 3 kg

2 8 kg **4** 6 kg **6** $\frac{1}{2}$ kg

Write as kilograms.

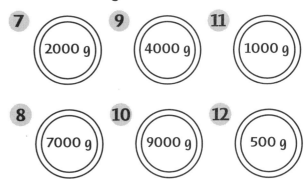

7 2000 g **9** 4000 g **11** 1000 g

8 7000 g **10** 9000 g **12** 500 g

Read the measurement shown on each scale.

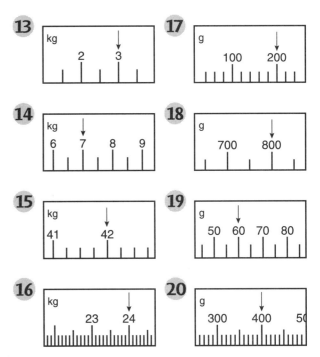

13 kg 2 3

17 g 100 200

14 kg 6 7 8 9

18 g 700 800

15 kg 41 42

19 g 50 60 70 80

16 kg 23 24

20 g 300 400 50

B

Copy and complete.

1. 4500 g = ☐ kg ☐ g = ☐ kg
2. 2500 g = ☐ kg ☐ g = ☐ kg
3. 1500 g = ☐ kg ☐ g = ☐ kg
4. 5000 g = ☐ kg ☐ g = ☐ kg
5. 2000 g = ☐ kg ☐ g = ☐ kg
6. 6500 g = ☐ kg ☐ g = ☐ kg
7. 3500 g = ☐ kg ☐ g = ☐ kg
8. 8500 g = ☐ kg ☐ g = ☐ kg

Would you use grams or kilograms to measure the weight of:

9. an exercise book
10. a lion
11. a lorry
12. a plastic football
13. a tin of beans
14. a lawn mower.

Read the measurement shown by the arrow on each dial.

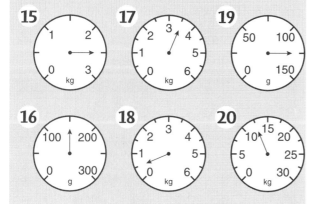

15. 16. 17. 18. 19. 20.

C

Write as grams.

1. 4.1 kg
2. 1.2 kg
3. 0.4 kg
4. 5.6 kg
5. 3.7 kg
6. 2.9 kg

Write as kilograms.

7. 3200 g
8. 4300 g
9. 1400 g
10. 2600 g
11. 5800 g
12. 900 g

Choose the more sensible of the two weights.

13. a CD → 70 g 700 g
14. a man → 7 kg 70 kg
15. a counter → 1 g 100 g
16. a car → 100 kg 1000 kg
17. a baby → 300 g 3 kg
18. an apple → 100 g 1 kg

Read the measurement shown by the arrow on each scale.

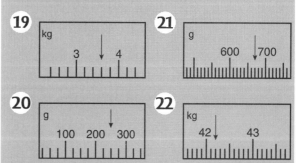

19. 20. 21. 22.

On these pages you will learn to use metric units of capacity.

Capacity is the amount of liquid that a container can hold.
The capacity of a bucket is greater than the capacity of a tea cup.

The metric units of capacity are litres and millilitres.

1000 ml = 1 litre

500 ml = half a litre

= 0·5 litres

100ml = 0·1 litres

2500 ml = 2·5 litres

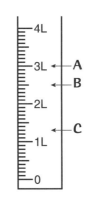

Examples

A = 3 litres

B = 2·5 litres

C = 1·3 litres

A

What is the capacity of these containers in litres?

1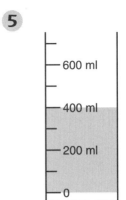

2000 millilitres

2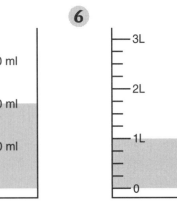

5000 millilitres

3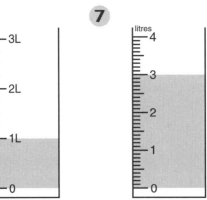

3000 millilitres

4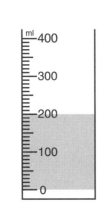

1000 millilitres

How much water is in each of these measuring flasks?

5

6

7

8

B

Copy and complete by filling in each box.

1 2500 ml = ☐ l ☐ ml = ☐ l   **4** 0·5 l = ☐ ml

2 3·5 l = ☐ l ☐ ml = ☐ ml   **5** 6000 ml = ☐ l

3 8500 ml = ☐ l ☐ ml = ☐ l   **6** 5·5 l = ☐ l ☐ ml = ☐ ml

Would you use litres or millilitres to measure the capacity of:

7 an egg cup   **9** a cereal bowl   **11** a paddling pool

8 a fish tank   **10** a mug   **12** a wine glass?

Read the measurement shown by each of the arrows.

13   **14**   **15**   **16**

C

Copy each sentence and choose the most sensible estimate.

1 A paper cup holds (2 ml, 20 ml, 200 ml) of water.

2 The capacity of a tablespoon is (10 ml, 100 ml, 1000 ml).

3 A can of cola contains (30 ml, 300 ml, 3000 ml).

4 A washing up bowl has a capacity of (500 ml, 5 l, 50 l).

For each of the scales work out:

a) the measurement shown by each of the arrows.

b) the difference between each pair of arrows.

5   **6**   **7**   **8**

On this page you will learn to solve problems involving mass.

A

1. Alex weighs 38 kg. His brother weighs 13 kg more. How much does Alex's brother weigh?

2. A box of apples weighs 6 kg. How much do 5 boxes weigh?

3. A sack has 43 kg of potatoes. 11 kg of potatoes are used. What is the weight of the potatoes left in the sack?

4. Jodie's mother weighs 60 kg. Jodie weighs half as much. How much does Jodie weigh?

5. A tile weighs 40 g. What is the weight of 10 tiles?

B

1. A tin of fish weighs 200 g. What do four tins weigh?

2. Molly buys 1 kg of carrots. 600 g are eaten. What is the weight of the carrots that are left?

3. A builder loads 43 kg of sand into his van. He adds 26 kg of cement. What is the combined weight of the sand and the cement?

4. A cake weighs one kg. It is cut into five equal slices. How much does each slice weigh?

5. Keith's father weighs 75 kg. Keith weighs 40 kg less. How much does Keith weigh?

C

1. Fifty dictionaries weigh 10 kg. How much does one dictionary weigh?

2. A bag contains 3 kg of flour. 1600 g is used. What is the weight of the flour left in the bag?

3. One tin of peas weighs 300 g. What do 8 tins weigh? Give your answer in kilograms and grams.

4. A small loaf weighs half a kilogram. It is cut into 10 equal slices. What does each slice weigh?

5. A parcel weighs one and a half kilograms. A second parcel weighs 800 g more. What is the combined weight of the parcels?

On this page you will learn to solve problems involving capacity.

A

1 A bottle of shampoo holds 200 ml. 80 ml is used. How much shampoo is there in the bottle?

2 There are 43 litres of water in a paddling pool. 15 litres is added. How much water is there now in the paddling pool?

3 There is 26 litres of water in a bath. Nine litres came from the cold water tap. How much water came from the hot water tap?

4 A shower uses 7 litres of water in one minute. How much water is used in five minutes?

5 A full fish tank holds 28 litres of water. The tank is only half full. How much water is in the tank?

B

1 3 children share 900 ml of lemonade. How much lemonade does each child have?

2 A jar of orange squash is made using 700 ml of water and 200 ml of orange. How much orange squash is there?

3 6 buckets are used to fill a fish tank. Each bucket holds 4 litres of water. How much water is there in the fish tank?

4 A shop has 58 litres of ice cream. 19 litres is sold. How much ice cream is left?

5 There is 150 ml of perfume in one bottle. How much perfume is there in four bottles?

C

1 A carton of cream contains 500 ml. How much cream is needed to fill 10 cartons? Give your answer in litres.

2 A container of milk holds 2 litres. 1200 ml is used. How much milk is left?

3 There is 2 litres of orange juice in a jar. It can fill 10 cups. How much orange juice can each cup hold?

4 There is half a litre of cold water in a bowl. 600 ml of hot water is added. How much water is there now in the bowl?

5 8 glasses can be filled from a bottle of cola. Each glass holds 250 ml. How much cola is in the bottle in litres?

On these pages you will learn to know and use the units of time and to use a calendar.

1 year = 365 days
     = 52 weeks
     = 12 months
1 day = 24 hours
1 hour = 60 minutes
1 minute = 60 seconds

DECEMBER						
Su	M	Tu	W	Th	F	Sa
	①1	2	3	4	5	6
7	8	9	10	11	12	13
14	15	16	17	18	19	20
21	22	23	24	㉕25	26	27
28	29	30	㉛31			

There are 31 days in December.
December 1st is a Monday.
Christmas Day is a Thursday.
New Year's Eve is a Wednesday.

Use a calendar.
Find out on which day Christmas Day falls this year.

A

Copy and complete by filling in the box.

1 1 day   = ☐ hours

2 1 hour   = ☐ minutes

3 1 minute   = ☐ seconds

4 1 week   = ☐ days

5 1 fortnight   = ☐ weeks

6 ☐ days   = 48 hours

7 ☐ weeks   = 21 days

8 ☐ minutes   = 120 seconds

9 ☐ fortnights = 8 weeks

10 ☐ weeks   = 70 days

11 The months of the year have been written in alphabetical order.
Write them out in their calendar order.

      April   February   June   November

      August   January   March   October

      December   July   May   September

12 What will be the date one week from today?

B

Copy and complete by filling in the box.

1. 1 year = ☐ days
2. 1 year = ☐ weeks
3. 5 weeks = ☐ days
4. 1 year = ☐ months
5. $\frac{1}{2}$ minute = ☐ seconds
6. ☐ years = 36 months
7. ☐ years = 104 weeks
8. ☐ weeks = 28 days
9. ☐ minutes = 180 seconds
10. ☐ minutes = 2 hours

Look at the calendar.

11. How many days are there in June?

12. On which day of the week falls:
    a) June 1st   c) June 6th
    b) June 17th   d) June 28th.

13. How many Sundays are there in the month?

14. How many Thursdays are there?

15. What is the date of the third Monday in the month?

16. Use a calendar to find out which months have:
    a) 31 days   b) 30 days   c) 28 or 29 days.

JUNE						
Su	M	Tu	W	Th	F	Sa
			1	2	3	4
5	6	7	8	9	10	11
12	13	14	15	16	17	18
19	20	21	22	23	24	25
26	27	28	29	30		

C

Write as minutes.

1. 10 hours
2. $2\frac{1}{2}$ hours
3. 600 seconds
4. 90 seconds

Write as days.

5. 6 weeks
6. 20 weeks
7. 12 hours
8. 120 hours

Write as years.

9. 48 months
10. 6 months
11. 520 weeks
12. 156 weeks.

Look at the calendar.

On which day of the week will these children have their birthdays?

13. Marsha   – 14th October
14. Brandon   – 11th October
15. Lauren   – 30th September
16. Samantha – 1st November
17. Ryan   – 18th November

OCTOBER						
Su	M	Tu	W	Th	F	Sa
		1	2	3	4	5
6	7	8	9	10	11	12
13	14	15	16	17	18	19
20	21	22	23	24	25	26
27	28	29	30	31		

On these pages you will learn to read the time, using a.m. and p.m.

Analogue clocks have faces.
Read the minutes as:
"past" before 30 minutes.
"to" after 30 minutes.

a.m. means before 12 noon.

Digital clocks have figures only.
The minutes are always shown as
minutes past the hour.

p.m. means after 12 noon.

Examples

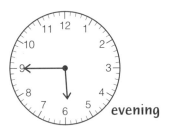

quarter to 6
5 : 45 p.m.

$\boxed{5:45}$

5 minutes past 7
7 : 05 a.m.

$\boxed{7:05}$

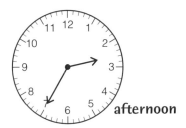

25 minutes to 3
2 : 35 p.m.

$\boxed{2:35}$

A

Write the time shown on each of these clocks in words.

5 $\boxed{6:15}$ **6** $\boxed{9:00}$ **7** $\boxed{2:45}$ **8** $\boxed{5:30}$

B

Write the times shown on these clocks:
a) in words
b) in figures, using a.m. and p.m..

1 morning

2 afternoon

3 morning

4 afternoon

5 8:55 evening

6 6:10 morning

7 10:40 night

8 3:20 night

9 What would be the time if each anologue clock was 30 minutes fast?

10 What would be the time if each digital clock was 5 minutes slow?

C

Write the times shown on these clocks:
a) in words
b) in figures, using a.m. and p.m..

1 afternoon

2 morning

3 night

4 evening

5 0:13 lunchtime

6 8:42 morning

7 1:29 afternoon

8 5:54 morning

9 What would the time be if each of the clocks was 5 minutes slow?

10 What would the time be if each of the clocks was 12 minutes fast?

On this page you will learn to solve problems involving time.

A

1 Chloe puts a cake in the oven at 4:45. She takes it out at 5:15. How long is the cake in the oven?

2 The lesson begins at 2:00. It lasts half an hour. At what time does the lesson finish?

3 It takes Carla 15 minutes to walk to the park. She sets off at 2:30. When does she arrive?

4 Paul went into the sea at 12:15. He came out 45 minutes later. At what time did he come out of the sea?

5 Sita reads for an hour. She starts reading at 6:15. At what time does she finish reading?

B

1 Cherie's favourite television programme starts at 6:40. It finishes at 7:20. How long is the programme?

2 Danny left school at 3:20. It took him 25 minutes to walk home. At what time did he arrive home?

3 Lunchtime lasts 50 minutes. It finishes at 1:00. When does it start?

4 A football game starts at 2:10. It lasts 35 minutes. When does it finish?

5 A clock shows the time as 10:20. The real time is 9:55. How many minutes fast is the clock?

C

1 The Gym Club lasts 70 minutes. It finishes at 4:30. When does it start?

2 The coach leaves school at 10:38. It arrives at the museum at 11.00. How long is the journey?

3 The P.E. lesson begins at 2:25. It lasts 45 minutes. When does it finish?

4 Mr Carter gets up at 7:10. He leaves for work 40 minutes later. His journey takes 30 minutes. When does he arrive at his office?

5 A film begins at 2:45. It finishes at 4:20. How long is the film.

A

Find the number.

1 between 20 and 30
the sum of its digits is 7

2 between 12 and 19
a multiple of 5

3 between 30 and 40
the product of its digits is 12

4 between 30 and 40
the sum of its digits is 11

5 between 25 and 30
a multiple of 4

6 between 70 and 80
the product of its digits is 21

B

Find the number:

1 a 2-digit number below 30
the sum of its digits is 4
the product of its digits is 3

2 a multiple of 9
between 20 and 50
an even number

3 a multiple of 8
a 2-digit number
the product of its digits is 14

4 above 30
the product of its digits is 8
a multiple of 6.

Find a pair of numbers with:

5 a sum of 8 and a product of 15

6 a sum of 8 and a product of 12

7 a sum of 7 and a product of 12

8 a sum of 19 and a product of 90

9 a sum of 6 and a product of 8

10 a sum of 13 and a product of 40.

TOP SECRET

C

Copy and complete the table. The first column has been done for you.

1st number	3	3	6						
2nd number	2			7	8	12			
Sum of numbers	5	12	11				13	15	15
Product of numbers	6			28	64	120	42	54	56

On these pages you will learn to name and classify 2-D shapes.

CURVED SHAPES

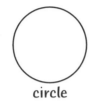

These shapes have curved edges.

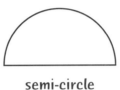

circle

semi-circle

TRIANGLES

2-D shapes with three straight edges are called triangles.

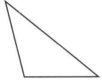

QUADRILATERALS

2-D shapes with four straight edges are called quadrilaterals.

squares are quadrilaterals

rectangles are quadrilaterals

POLYGONS

2-D shapes with more than four straight edges have special names.

5 sides

pentagon

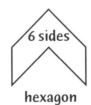

6 sides

hexagon

8 sides

octagon

Here are some shapes.

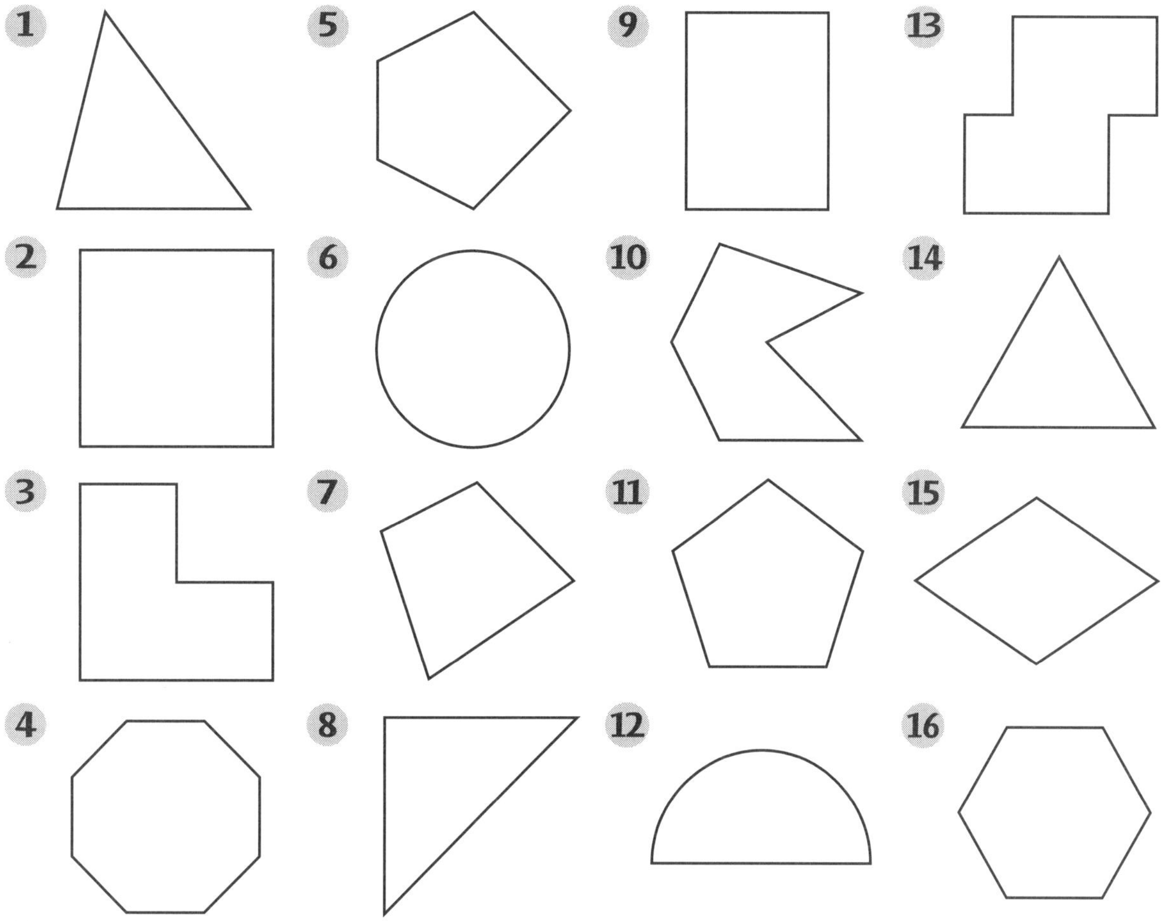

1 **5** **9** **13**

2 **6** **10** **14**

3 **7** **11** **15**

4 **8** **12** **16**

A

Write the name of each of the shapes.

B

Copy and complete the table for each of the shapes.

Number	Edges	Shape
1	3	triangle

C

Sort the above shapes into both Carroll Diagrams by writing the number of each shape in the right place.

1

	4 edges	not 4 edges
equal sides		
not equal sides		

(Leave out shapes 6 and 12.)

2

	not symmetrical	symmetrical
1 or more right angles		
no right angles		

On these pages you will learn to name and classify 3-D shapes.

Some 3-D shapes with curved faces.

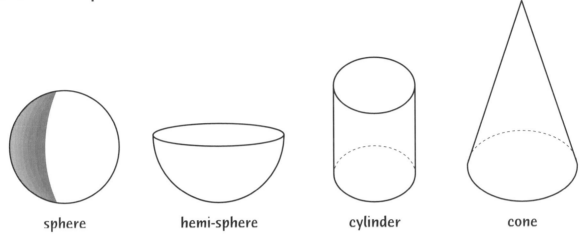

sphere   hemi-sphere   cylinder   cone

Some 3-D shapes with straight edges.

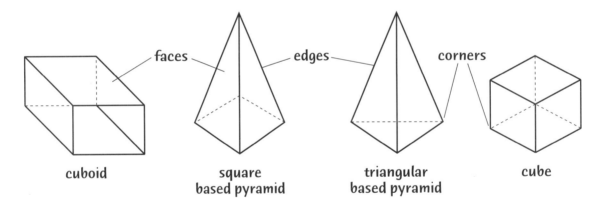

faces   edges   corners

cuboid   square based pyramid   triangular based pyramid   cube

A prism is a 3-D shape with two identical end faces and the same cross section throughout its length.

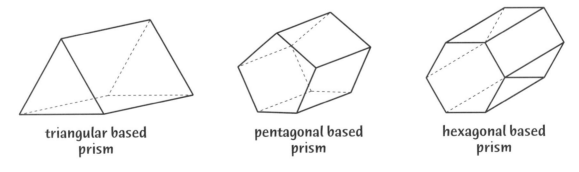

triangular based prism   pentagonal based prism   hexagonal based prism

Here are some shapes.

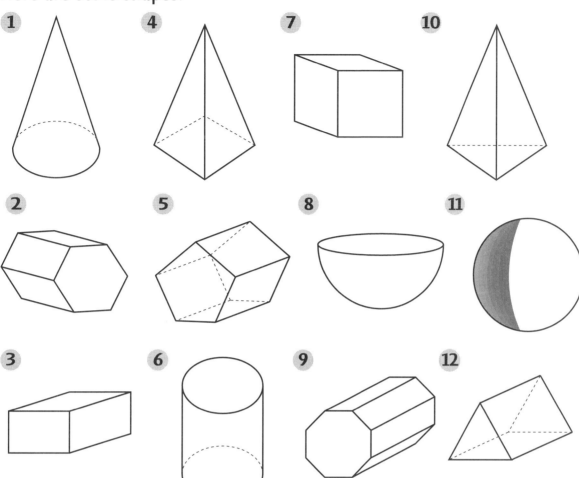

A

Write the name of each of the shapes.

B

Write the names of:

1 4 shapes with curved faces
2 2 shapes with 8 corners
3 1 shape with 10 corners
4 2 shapes with 5 flat faces

5 2 shapes with 1 circular flat face
6 1 shape with 8 faces
7 1 shape with 6 edges
8 1 shape with 24 edges.

C

Copy and complete the table for each of the shapes.

No.	Shape	Flat faces	Edges	Corners
1	cone	2	1	1
2	hexagonal prism	8	18	12

On this page you will explore putting identical shapes together to make new shapes.

1 Start with a rectangle of card.

Draw a line to join the midway points of the shorter sides.

Cut the rectangle into 2 halves.

2 Put the shapes together to make:

a) a rectangle
b) a hexagon
c) three different octagons.
Do not overlap the shapes.

Example

octagon

3 Draw round and name your shapes.

B

1 Cut a rectangle of card into 2 equal triangles.

2 Put your shapes together to make:

a) 2 different triangles
b) 3 different quadrilaterals
c) 2 different pentagons
d) 2 different hexagons.

3 Draw round and name your shapes.

1 Cut a square of card into 4 equal triangles.

2 Using all four triangles can you make:

a) a triangle?
b) 4 different quadrilaterals?

3 Explore the different pentagons, hexagons and octagons that you can make by putting together all four triangles.

4 Draw round and name your shapes.

On this page you will learn to relate 3-D shapes to pictures of them.

1

5

9

13

2

6

10

14

3

7

11

15

4

8

12

16

A

Use cubes to build these shapes.

B

Without using cubes, work out how many cubes are needed to build these shapes.

Example

6 cubes are needed.
(Only 5 cubes can be seen.)

C

How many more cubes are needed to turn each shape into a cuboid?

Example

2 cubes are needed.

On these pages you will learn to recognise line symmetry in 2-D shapes.

A shape is symmetrical if half of its shape matches the other half exactly. The line separating the two halves is the line of symmetry or mirror line.

Examples

One line
of symmetry

One line
of symmetry

Two lines
of symmetry

Two lines
of symmetry

A

Copy the shapes. Draw on one line of symmetry.

1

3

5

2

4
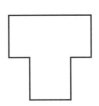

6
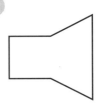

7 Copy the letters. Draw on one line of symmetry.

B

Copy the shapes onto squared paper.
Draw two lines of symmetry on each shape.

1 4 7 10

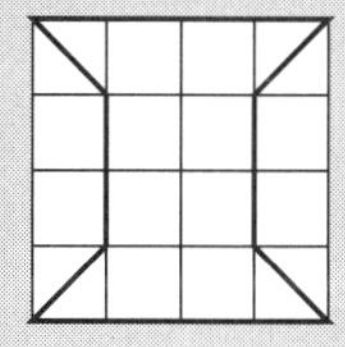

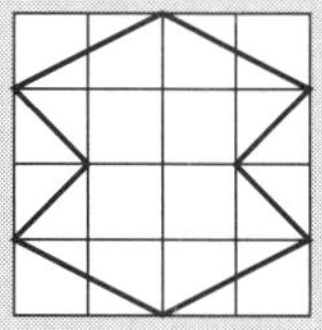

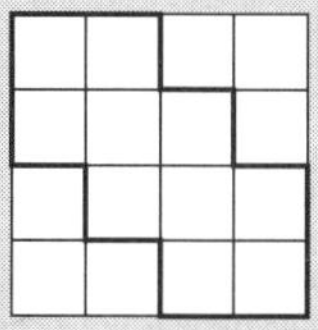

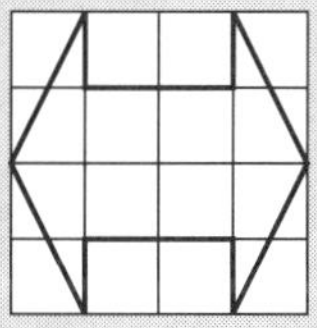

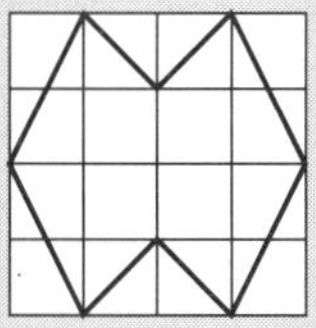

2 5 8 11

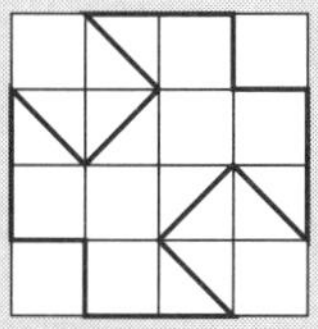

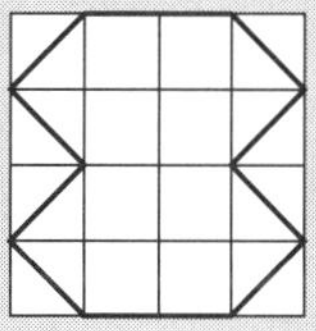

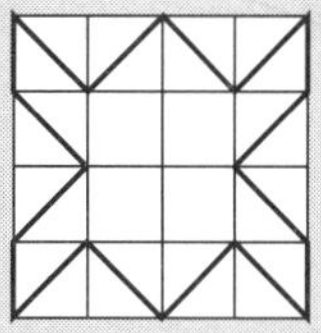

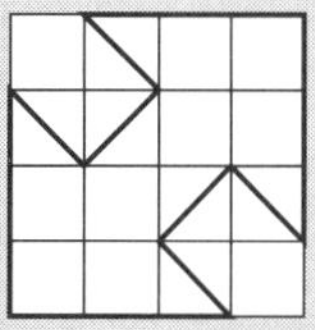

3 6 9 12

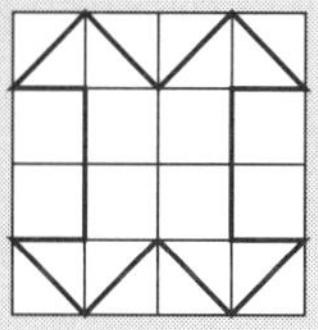

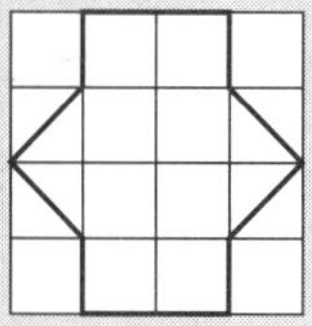

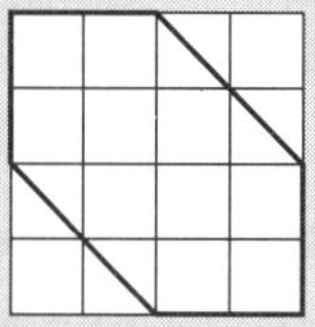

C

Copy the patterns below onto squared paper. Shade in as many squares as necessary to complete the symmetrical patterns.

1 2 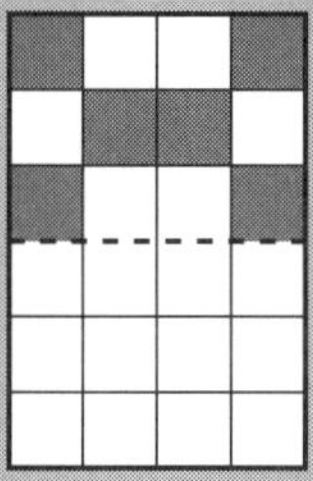 3 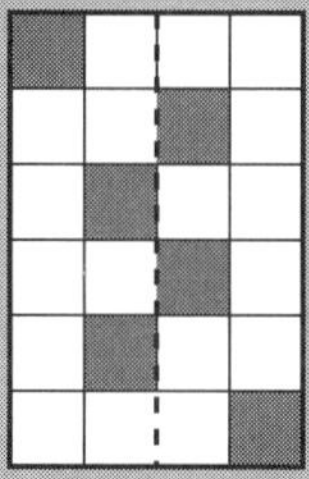 4

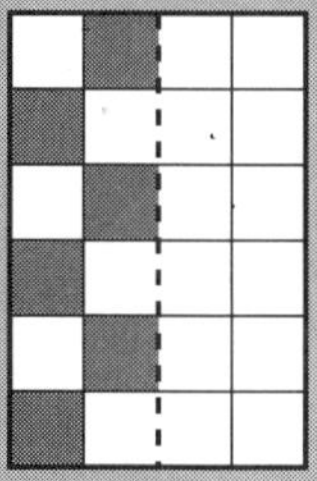

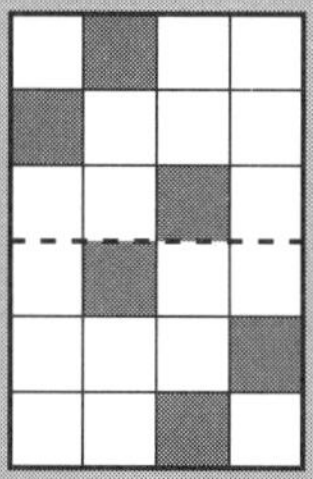

5 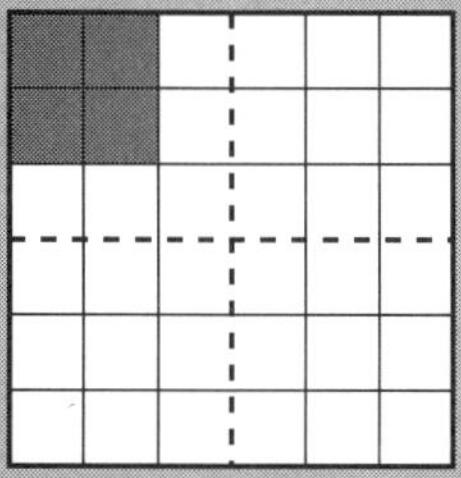 6 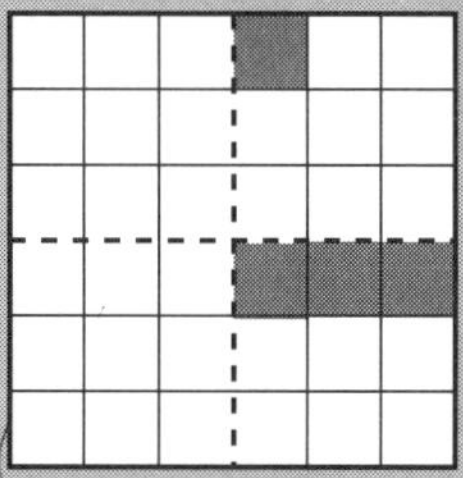 7

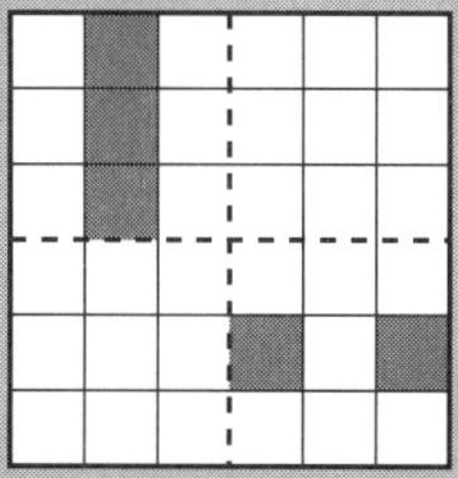

8 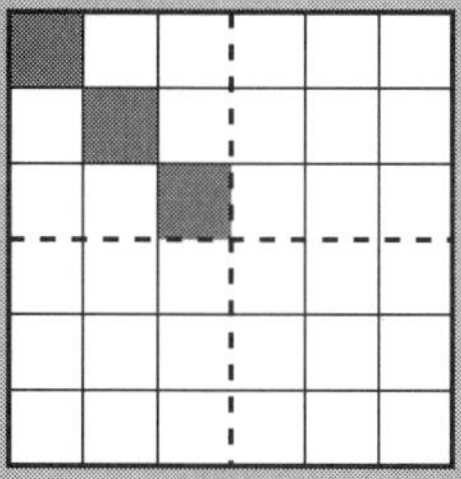 9 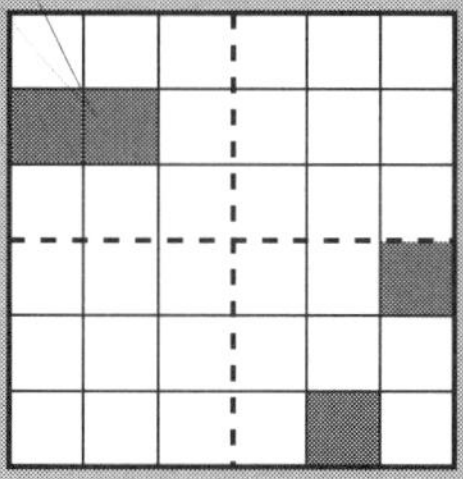 10

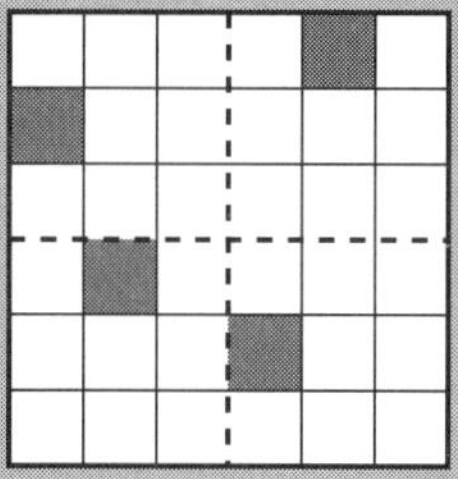

On these pages you will learn to find the position of a square on a grid and use the four compass directions.

Examples

The ○ is in square C4.

The □ is in square A3.

The △ is in square D2.

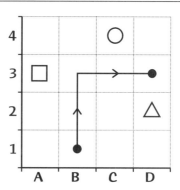

Start at B1.
Go North 2 squares.
Go East 2 squares.
Finish at square D3.

A

The numbers 1, 2, 3, 4 . . . are written in a spiral.

1 Count clockwise 4 squares from 3.

2 Count clockwise 6 squares from 9.

3 Count anti-clockwise 5 squares from 19.

4 Count anti-clockwise 7 squares from 11.

5 Which number is just below:

a) 20   b) 2   c) 13?

6 Which 4 numbers are next to:

a) 8   b) 16   c) 1?

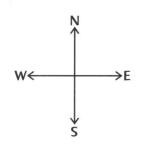

36	17	18	19	20	21
35	16	5	6	7·	22
34	15	4	1	8	23
33	14	3	2	9	24
32	13	12	11	10	25
31	30	29	28	27	26

Start at 1. Follow the directions. Where do you finish?

7 Up 2 squares.
Left 2 squares.

8 Down 3 squares.
Right 1 square.

9 Down 2 squares.
Left 3 squares.

This time start at 3 and follow the directions. Where do you finish?

10 Up 2 squares.
Right 3 squares.

11 Left 1 square
Down 2 squares.

12 Right 2 squares.
Up 3 squares.

B

Give the positions of these symbols:

1 ◇   4 ⊞   7 ▲

2 ⊖   5 ◇   8 □

3 △   6 ⊕   9 ●

Draw the symbol which is found on each of these squares.

10 E4   13 E3   16 A4

11 A2   14 D3   17 B2

12 C1   15 C5   18 D4

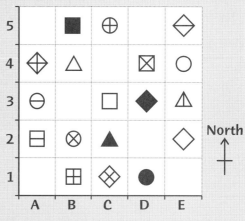

North

Follow the directions. Draw the symbol you come to.

19 Start at B5.
   South 3 squares.
   East 3 squares.

20 Start at A2.
   East 4 squares
   North 3 squares.

21 Start at D4.
   West 3 squares.
   South 2 squares.

22 Start at D1.
   North 4 squares.
   West 2 squares.

23 Start at E5.
   South 3 squares.
   West 4 squares.

24 Start at B2.
   North 2 squares.
   East 2 squares.

C

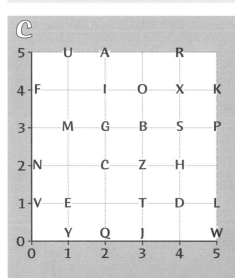

The position of a point on a grid is given by its co-ordinates. The across co-ordinate always comes first.

Examples

Point M is (1, 3).   Point Q is (2, 0).
Point T is (3, 1).   Point N is (0, 2).

1 Use the grid to spell out this message. Read across.

(5, 0)(4, 2)(1, 1)(0, 2)   (1, 0)(3, 4)(1, 5)   (0, 4)(2, 4)(0, 2)(4, 1)   (2, 5)
(5, 3)(3, 4)(4, 3)(2, 4)(3, 1)(2, 4)(3, 4)(0, 2)   (3, 4)(0, 2)   (2, 5)
(2, 3)(4, 5)(2, 4)(4, 1)   (2, 3)(3, 4)   (2, 5)(2, 2)(4, 5)(3, 4)(4, 3)(4, 3)
(0, 4)(2, 4)(4, 5)(4, 3)(3, 1)   (2, 5)(0, 2)(4, 1)   (3, 1)(4, 2)(1, 1)(0, 2)
(2, 3)(3, 4)   (1, 5)(5, 3).

2 Write your name and the name of your school in co-ordinates.

On these pages you will learn to recognise whole, half and quarter turns.

A $\frac{1}{2}$ turn is a straight line.　　　A $\frac{1}{4}$ turn is a right angle.

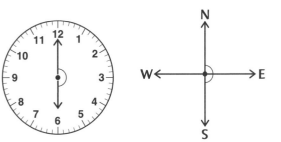　　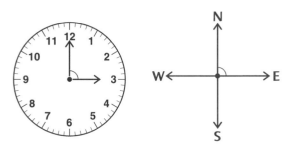

The minute hand of a clock makes:

a whole turn in one hour

a half turn in 30 minutes

a quarter turn in 15 minutes.

A compass turning clockwise from:

N to N is a whole turn

N to S is a half turn

N to E is a quarter turn.

Find the new time if the hour hand of a clock makes these turns from:

| 12 o' clock | 4 o' clock | 11 o' clock |

1 a whole turn　　　　**4** a half turn　　　　**7** a quarter turn

2 a half turn　　　　　**5** a quarter turn　　　**8** a whole turn

3 a quarter turn　　　**6** a whole turn　　　　**9** a half turn.

Are these compass movements half or quarter turns?

10 S to N　　　**12** E to W　　　**14** E to S　　　**16** W to E

11 N to E　　　**13** W to N　　　**15** N to S　　　**17** S to W

Are these angles right angles? Write Yes or No.

18　　　　**19**　　　　**20**　　　　**21**

B

Write down whether each of the angles of these shapes is:
a) a right angle
b) greater than a right angle
c) less than a right angle.

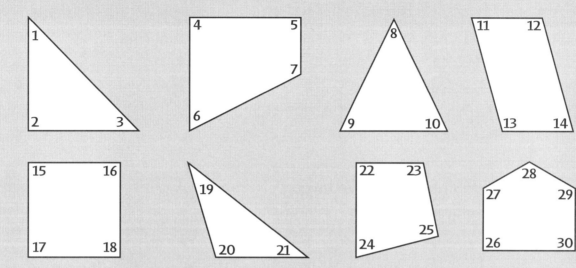

C

Angles are measured in degrees (°).

A whole turn is 360°.
A half turn is 180°.
A quarter turn is 90°.

Find the time if the hour hand turns these angles from:

12 o' clock	2 o' clock	7 o' clock	11 o' clock
1 360°	**5** 360°	**9** 180°	**13** 360°
2 180°	**6** 90°	**10** 90°	**14** 180°
3 90°	**7** 30°	**11** 30°	**15** 90°
4 30°	**8** 60°	**12** 120°	**16** 270°.

How many degrees is the turn clockwise from:

17 S to N **21** E to S
18 N to E **22** N to W
19 E to W **23** W to N
20 W to S **24** S to E.

How many degrees is the turn anticlockwise from:

25 S to E **29** E to W
26 N to S **30** S to W
27 E to N **31** W to S
28 W to N **32** N to E.

On these pages you will learn to use Carroll diagrams or Venn diagrams to sort numbers or shapes.

Examples

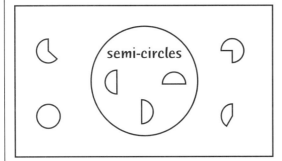

These shapes have been sorted into a Venn diagram.

The multiples of 3 up to 30 have been sorted into the Carroll diagram.

even	not even
6	3
12	9
18	15
24	21
30	27

Look at the numbers in the ring.

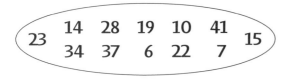

1 Make a list of the numbers which are above 20.

2 Make a list of the numbers which are even numbers.

3 Which numbers are in both lists?

4 Make a list of the shapes which are triangles.

5 Make a list of the shapes which have at least one right angle.

6 Which shapes are in both lists?

B

1 Copy the Carroll diagram.
Use it to sort the multiples of 5 up to 50.

5 10 15 20 25
30 35 40 45 50

odd numbers	not odd numbers

2 Copy the Venn diagram.
Sort the shapes by writing the letters in the right places.

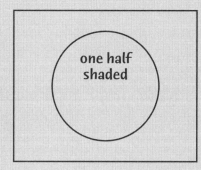 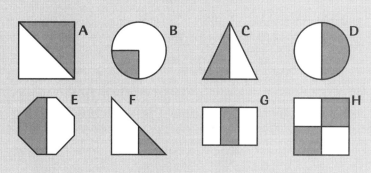

C

1 Copy the Venn diagram.
Use it to sort the numbers in the ring.

45 36 20 30 48
60 75 40 16 24

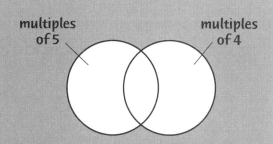

2 Copy the Carroll diagram.
Sort the shapes by writing the letters in the right places.

	symmetrical	not symmetrical
quadrilaterals		
not quadrilaterals		

On these pages you will learn:

- to make a frequency table.
- to make and interpret a bar chart.

Example

The ages of children in a basketball club.

```
10   9   8  10   9  10  11
 8  10  11   9  10   8  10
 9  10  10   8  11  10   9
10  11   9  10   8   9  10
```

A frequency table showing the ages.

Ages	No. of children
8	5
9	7
10	12
11	4

The data in the frequency table can be displayed in a bar chart.

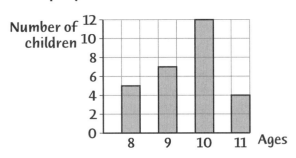

A

1 Class 3 were asked to choose their favourite lesson. The frequency table shows the results.

Subject	Votes
English	5
Maths	7
P.E.	8
Art	6

Draw a block graph to show the results.

2 This block graph shows the number of children absent from school each day in Year 3.

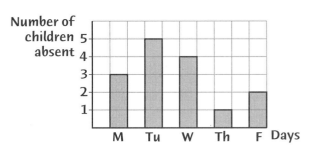

a) On which day were most children absent?

b) On which day were least children absent?

c) How many children were absent on Monday?

d) How many more children were absent on Wednesday than on Friday?

e) How many fewer children were absent on Monday than on Tuesday?

B

1 The members of a football club voted for the colour of their new kit. They chose from red, blue, gold and white. These are the results of the vote.

G B G R W G B R
R W R G G B R G
G R G B R W G R
B G W R G R B G

Make a frequency table and then draw a bar chart to show the results.

2 This graph shows the passengers on a bus.

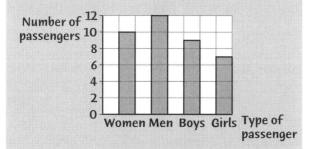

a) How many women were on the bus?
b) How many boys were on the bus?
c) How many adults were on the bus?
d) How many more women than girls were passengers?
e) How many fewer boys than men were passengers?
f) How many passengers were there altogether?

C

1 The children in Year 3 were asked how they came to school. It was found that they walked or came by car, bus or train. These are the results.

C B W C T W C C
C W C B W C T W
B C T C W W B C
C C W W C B C W
C W B C T C W C

Make a frequency table and then draw a bar chart to show the results.

2 This graph shows the number of children walking to school in each year group.

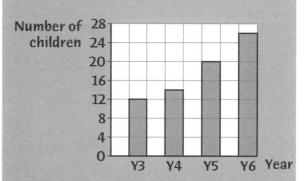

a) How many children walked to school in Year 4?
b) How many more children walked to school in Year 5 than in Year 3?
c) How many children walked to school altogether?
d) In which Year did most children walk to school? Why do you think this was?

On these pages you will learn to make and use a pictogram.

Example

The flowers in a display were the following numbers of blue, white, yellow and red flowers.

R   Y   W   R   B   Y   R   R
Y   R   B   Y   W   R   Y   W
R   Y   Y   W   R   Y   B   R
R   W   R   B   Y   W   R   Y

A frequency table showing the colours.

Colours	Number of flowers
Blue	4
Red	12
White	6
Yellow	10

The data in the frequency table can be displayed in a pictogram.

Blue   🌼 🌼

Red   🌼 🌼 🌼 🌼 🌼

White   🌼 🌼 🌼

Yellow   🌼 🌼 🌼 🌼

🌼 represents 2 flowers

A

1 In one day a shop sold these numbers of black, red, white and yellow T-vests.

W   B   W   Y   B   W   R   W
W   Y   W   B   W   B   Y   B
B   W   R   W   B   Y   B   W

Make a frequency table and then draw a pictogram to show the results.

2 This pictogram shows the types of birds seen in a garden.

Blackbirds   ⌒ ⌒ ⌒ ⌒

Sparrows   ⌒ ⌒ ⌒ ⌒ ⌒ ⌒

Starlings   ⌒ ⌒ ⌒ ⌒ ⌒ ⌒ ⌒

Thrushes   ⌒ ⌒ ⌒

⌒ represents 1 bird

a) Which type of bird was seen most often?
b) Which type of bird was seen least often?
c) How many blackbirds were seen in the garden?
d) How many more sparrows than blackbirds were seen in the garden?
e) How many birds were seen in the garden altogether?

B

1 The children on a school trip had brought these numbers of apple, blackcurrant, cola and orange drinks.

```
C C B O B A C B
O C O C O B O A
C O B A C O C C
C O C O B A C O
```

Make a frequency table and then draw a pictogram to show the results.

2 This pictogram shows the type of shoes worn to school by children in Year 1.

ⵊ represents 2 children

a) How many children wore boots?

b) What was the most common type of shoe?

c) What was the least common type of shoe?

d) How many fewer children wore boots than trainers?

e) How many children are there in Year 1?

C

1 In one day a sweet shop sold these numbers of packets of chocolate, fruit, mint and toffee sweets.

```
T C F C T M C T F C
C F M T C F C M T F
M C F C T T F C M T
T F C M C T M F T C
T C F M C F T T F C
```

Make a frequency table and then draw a pictogram to show the results.

2 This pictogram shows the number of snails found by a gardener on his cabbages.

ⵊ represents 5 snails

a) How many snails were found on Thursday?

b) How many more snails were found on Thursday than on Friday?

c) How many fewer snails were found on Saturday than on Wednesday?

d) How many snails were found altogether?

e) On which day were least snails found?
Can you explain why?

Write in words.

1 57 **5** 725

2 183 **6** 206

3 340 **7** 494

4 612 **8** 879

Give the value of the underlined digit.

9 14<u>2</u> **13** <u>7</u>26

10 6<u>3</u>8 **14** 56<u>3</u>

11 20<u>5</u> **15** 91<u>7</u>

12 4<u>9</u>1 **16** <u>3</u>89

Count on in 10s:

17 50 from 136

18 30 from 340

19 60 from 508

20 40 from 251.

Count back in 10s:

21 40 from 273

22 50 from 465

23 70 from 592

24 60 from 874.

Count on in 100s:

25 300 from 634

26 600 from 278

27 500 from 122

28 700 from 257.

Copy the sequence. Write the next three numbers.

29 7 9 11 13

30 25 22 19 16

31 11 21 31 41

32 35 30 25 20

33 10 14 18 22

34 25 28 31 34

35 26 24 22 20

36 12 17 22 27

37 40 36 32 28

38 50 100 150

Which number is smaller?

39 213 or 231

40 682 or 628

41 735 or 753

Write in order. Start with largest.

42 275 572 752 257

43 894 948 849 489

44 136 361 163 316

Round to the nearest:

(10)   (100)

45 23   **49** 160

46 57   **50** 340

47 72   **51** 650

48 45   **52** 874.

Estimate the numbers shown by the arrows.

53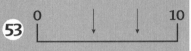

54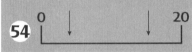

55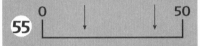

56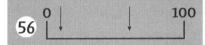

Write odd or even for each of these numbers.

57 23   **61** 30

58 16   **62** 49

59 85   **63** 7

60 14   **64** 72.

Write the first four multiples of:

65 3   **67** 20

66 11   **68** 6.

| 30 | 28 | 21 | 20 |
| 27 | 15 | 50 | 35 |

Write the numbers in the box which are multiples of:

69 2   **71** 3

70 5   **72** 10.

What fraction of each shape is shaded?

1

2

3

4

5

6

7

8

What fractions are shown by the arrows?

9

10

11

12

Use the fraction charts to copy and complete the equivalent fractions.

13 $1 = \dfrac{\square}{5}$

14 $\dfrac{1}{4} = \dfrac{\square}{8}$

15 $\dfrac{1}{2} = \dfrac{\square}{10}$

16 $1 = \dfrac{\square}{8}$

17 $\dfrac{3}{4} = \dfrac{\square}{8}$

18 $\dfrac{1}{5} = \dfrac{\square}{10}$

19 $\dfrac{1}{2} = \dfrac{\square}{4}$

20 $1 = \dfrac{\square}{10}$

21 $\dfrac{4}{5} = \dfrac{\square}{10}$

22 $\dfrac{1}{2} = \dfrac{\square}{8}$

Find one half of:

23 20

24 12

25 18

26 24

27 16

28 28

29 14

30 30.

Find one quarter of:

31 8 cm

32 28 cm

33 16 cm

34 20 cm

35 12 cm

36 40 cm

37 24 cm

38 32 cm.

Find one tenth of:

39 10p

40 £1

41 50p

42 20p

43 40p

44 70p

45 30p

46 90p.

47 There are 40 children born in a hospital. Half of them are boys. How many are girls?

48 There are 36 biscuits in a tin. One quarter of them are eaten. How many are left?

Copy and complete.

1. $35 + 17$
2. $46 + 300$
3. $1000 - 300$
4. $80 + 45$
5. $78 - 21$
6. $1200 - 500$
7. $100 - 55$
8. $68 - 32$
9. $1000 - 600$
10. $200 - 192$
11. $34 + 19$
12. $256 + 70$

Work out:

13.
$$\begin{array}{r} 73 \\ + 65 \\ \hline \end{array}$$

17.
$$\begin{array}{r} 91 \\ - 44 \\ \hline \end{array}$$

14.
$$\begin{array}{r} 64 \\ + 28 \\ \hline \end{array}$$

18.
$$\begin{array}{r} 68 \\ - 35 \\ \hline \end{array}$$

15.
$$\begin{array}{r} 53 \\ + 27 \\ \hline \end{array}$$

19.
$$\begin{array}{r} 82 \\ - 63 \\ \hline \end{array}$$

16.
$$\begin{array}{r} 92 \\ + 76 \\ \hline \end{array}$$

20.
$$\begin{array}{r} 70 \\ - 26 \\ \hline \end{array}$$

Copy and complete.

21.

+	19	26	31
27			
30		56	
45			76

Double these numbers.

22. 20
23. 800
24. 65
25. 17

Halve these numbers.

26. 140
27. 36
28. 700
29. 190

Copy and complete.

30.

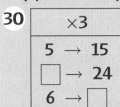

×3
5 → 15
☐ → 24
6 → ☐

31.

×4
8 → ☐
☐ → 36
6 → ☐

Copy and complete.

32. $7 \times 4 = \square$
33. $9 \times 3 = \square$
34. $5 \times \square = 40$
35. $10 \times \square = 60$
36. $\square \times 8 = 8$
37. $\square \times 3 = 21$
38. $16 \div 2 = \square$
39. $45 \div 5 = \square$
40. $30 \div \square = 5$
41. $7 \div \square = 1$
42. $\square \div 8 = 3$
43. $\square \div 4 = 5$

Copy and complete by writing the remainder.

44. $48 \div 5 = 9$ r. $\square$
45. $19 \div 3 = 6$ r. $\square$
46. $30 \div 4 = 7$ r. $\square$
47. $87 \div 10 = 8$ r. $\square$

48. There are 28 children in 4W and 26 in 4H. How many children are there in both classes?

49. There are 32 chocolates in a box. Half of them are eaten. How many chocolates are left?

50. Lee's book has 80 pages. He reads page 35. How many pages does he still have to read?

51. There are 4 tins in each pack. How many tins are there in 8 packs?

52. How many groups of 3 can be made from 26 children? How many children are left over?

Make 1 metre.

1 50 cm + ☐

2 85 cm + ☐

3 35 cm + ☐

4 55 cm + ☐

Make 1 km.

5 800 m + ☐

6 100 m + ☐

7 400 m + ☐

8 700 m + ☐

Write as grams.

9 3 kg   100 g

10 2.5 kg

Write as litres.

11 4000 ml

12 7500 ml

Work out the measurement shown by each arrow.

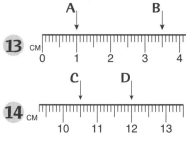

13

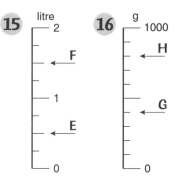

14

15

16

17 A piece of wood is 90 cm long. It is sawn in half. How long is each piece?

18 A bottle holds 800 ml of water. 300 ml is poured out. How much water is left?

19 A bag of potatoes weighs 5 kg. How much do 6 bags weigh?

20 Sam walks 28 km on Saturday and 19 km on Sunday. How far does he walk altogether?

Write as minutes.

21 30 seconds

22 2 hours

Write as days.

23 10 weeks

24 48 hours

Write as weeks.

25 1 year

26 21 days

Write the times shown:
a) in words
b) in figures, using a.m. and p.m..

27 afternoon

28 morning

29 `6:25` evening

30 `2:15` night

MARCH						
Su	M	Tu	W	Th	F	Sa
	1	2	3	4	5	6
7	8	9	10	11	12	13
14	15	16	17	18	19	20
21	22	23	24	25	26	27
28	29	30	31			

31 How many days are there in March?

32 How many Tuesdays are there in the month shown in the calendar.

33 On which day of the week does March 19th fall?

34 A lesson starts at 9:45. It lasts 35 minutes. At what time does the lesson finish?

Write the names of each of these 2-D shapes.

1

2

3

4

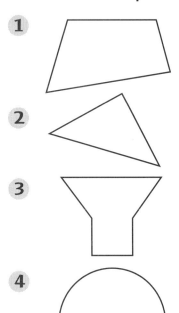

Use squared paper. Copy the shapes. Draw on two lines of symmetry on each shape.

5

6

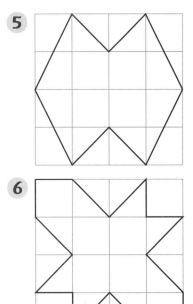

Write the names of each of these 3-D shapes.

7

8

9

10

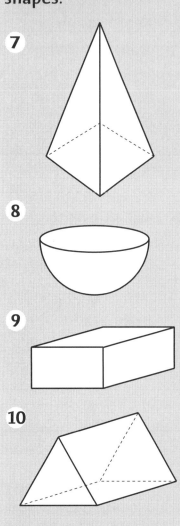

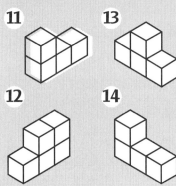

How many cubes are needed to build each shape?

11   **13**

12   **14**

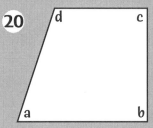

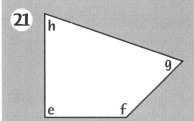

15 Give the position of all eight symbols.

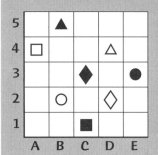

Which symbol is found:

16 North of ○
17 East of □
18 South of △
19 West of ● ?

Write down whether each of the angles is:
a) a right angle
b) less than a right angle
c) greater than a right angle.

20

d   c

a   b

21

h

g

e   f

1 Copy the Carroll diagram and use it to sort these numbers.

34 15 12 7 28
4 63 49 10 21

even numbers	not even numbers

2 Copy the Venn diagram and write the letters in the correct places.

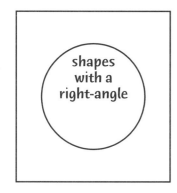

shapes with a right-angle

3 This bar chart shows the number of children in Class 3 having a school dinner in one week.

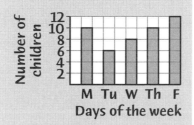

For each day of the week work out how many children had a school dinner.

4 A class voted for their favourite topic. They chose from Air, Egypt, Ponds and Food. These are the results.

E P F E P E A
P E A F E F P
F E P P A F E
E P F A P E E

Make a frequency table and draw a bar chart to show the results.

5 This pictogram shows the number of lollies sold by a shop.

Friday
Saturday
Sunday
Monday

🍦 shows 10 lollies

How many lollies were sold on the four days altogether?

6 Class 3 found that all the cars in a car park were red, blue, white or yellow. These are the results of their survey.

R W B W R Y R B
B W Y R B W W R
W B R W R W Y W
R W W Y W R B R

Make a frequency table and draw a pictogram to show the results.

TEST 1.

1. Write two hundred and fifty-eight in figures.
2. Add 35 to 400.
3. Round 760 to the nearest 100.
4. What is 7 times 5?
5. Write 312 pence as pounds and pence.
6. Take 19 from 65.
7. How many metres make one kilometre?
8. Share 18 by 3.
9. A carton of milk contains one litre. 300 ml is used. How much milk is left?
10. What is 400 more than 230?
11. Double 45.
12. How many days are there in five weeks?
13. How many boxes of four can be made from 24 balls?
14. Holly has two pounds. She spends £1·40. How much has she left?
15. How many quarters make a whole one?
16. Write two and half litres in millilitres.
17. What is 36 divided by 4?
18. Saheed has 77 marbles. Ryan has 43 marbles less than Saheed. How many marbles does Ryan have?

TEST 2

1. What is the difference between 65 and 100?
2. How many 50 pence pieces make £10.
3. What is seven multiplied by three?
4. Write five hundred and seven in figures.
5. What is the sum of 43 and 25?
6. What is one half of 700?
7. How many grams are there in one and a half kilograms?
8. A television programme starts at 8:10. It lasts 35 minutes. When does it finish?
9. What is 3 less than 400?
10. What is one tenth of 30 pence?
11. Round 68 to the nearest 10.
12. Find the product of 8 and 4.
13. What is 19 more than 27?
14. 25 centimetres is cut from one metre of wood. How much wood is left?
15. What is the cost of five pens at 30 pence each?
16. How many minutes are there in ten hours?
17. How many groups of three can be made from 24 children?
18. There are 58 children in a swimming pool. 21 are boys. How many are girls?

Example

4	9	2
3	5	7
8	1	6

In a magic square the sum of each row, column and diagonal is the same.

(↔) Rows (↔)	(↕) Columns (↕)	(↗) Diagonals (↘)
$4 + 9 + 2 = 15$	$4 + 3 + 8 = 15$	$4 + 5 + 6 = 15$
$3 + 5 + 7 = 15$	$9 + 5 + 1 = 15$	$8 + 5 + 2 = 15$
$8 + 1 + 6 = 15$	$2 + 7 + 6 = 15$	

Copy and complete the magic squares.

A

1

6	5	
11		
4		

2

3	10	5
	2	

3

6		
	5	
	3	4

B

1

3		
	8	
7		13

2

		10
		3
	5	14

3

	14	
11	6	13

C

1

16		
8		
15		10

2

12	16	
20		
13		

3

		11
	12	8
13		

How to learn a times table.

BY YOURSELF

1 Read the table over and over.
2 Cover the table and say it out loud or in your mind.
3 Say it more and more quickly.
4 Try to say the table backwards.

WITH A FRIEND

Ask each other questions like:
What is 6 times 4?
Multiply 4 by 7.
How many fours make 32?
Divide 36 by 4.

$1 \times 1 = 1$	$1 \times 2 = 2$	$1 \times 3 = 3$	$1 \times 4 = 4$	$1 \times 5 = 5$
$2 \times 1 = 2$	$2 \times 2 = 4$	$2 \times 3 = 6$	$2 \times 4 = 8$	$2 \times 5 = 10$
$3 \times 1 = 3$	$3 \times 2 = 6$	$3 \times 3 = 9$	$3 \times 4 = 12$	$3 \times 5 = 15$
$4 \times 1 = 4$	$4 \times 2 = 8$	$4 \times 3 = 12$	$4 \times 4 = 16$	$4 \times 5 = 20$
$5 \times 1 = 5$	$5 \times 2 = 10$	$5 \times 3 = 15$	$5 \times 4 = 20$	$5 \times 5 = 25$
$6 \times 1 = 6$	$6 \times 2 = 12$	$6 \times 3 = 18$	$6 \times 4 = 24$	$6 \times 5 = 30$
$7 \times 1 = 7$	$7 \times 2 = 14$	$7 \times 3 = 21$	$7 \times 4 = 28$	$7 \times 5 = 35$
$8 \times 1 = 8$	$8 \times 2 = 16$	$8 \times 3 = 24$	$8 \times 4 = 32$	$8 \times 5 = 40$
$9 \times 1 = 9$	$9 \times 2 = 18$	$9 \times 3 = 27$	$9 \times 4 = 36$	$9 \times 5 = 45$
$10 \times 1 = 10$	$10 \times 2 = 20$	$10 \times 3 = 30$	$10 \times 4 = 40$	$10 \times 5 = 50$

$1 \times 6 = 6$	$1 \times 7 = 7$	$1 \times 8 = 8$	$1 \times 9 = 9$	$1 \times 10 = 10$
$2 \times 6 = 12$	$2 \times 7 = 14$	$2 \times 8 = 16$	$2 \times 9 = 18$	$2 \times 10 = 20$
$3 \times 6 = 18$	$3 \times 7 = 21$	$3 \times 8 = 24$	$3 \times 9 = 27$	$3 \times 10 = 30$
$4 \times 6 = 24$	$4 \times 7 = 28$	$4 \times 8 = 32$	$4 \times 9 = 36$	$4 \times 10 = 40$
$5 \times 6 = 30$	$5 \times 7 = 35$	$5 \times 8 = 40$	$5 \times 9 = 45$	$5 \times 10 = 50$
$6 \times 6 = 36$	$6 \times 7 = 42$	$6 \times 8 = 48$	$6 \times 9 = 54$	$6 \times 10 = 60$
$7 \times 6 = 42$	$7 \times 7 = 49$	$7 \times 8 = 56$	$7 \times 9 = 63$	$7 \times 10 = 70$
$8 \times 6 = 48$	$8 \times 7 = 56$	$8 \times 8 = 64$	$8 \times 9 = 72$	$8 \times 10 = 80$
$9 \times 6 = 54$	$9 \times 7 = 63$	$9 \times 8 = 72$	$9 \times 9 = 81$	$9 \times 10 = 90$
$10 \times 6 = 60$	$10 \times 7 = 70$	$10 \times 8 = 80$	$10 \times 9 = 90$	$10 \times 10 = 100$